T0097755

EUGENE ENGLAND

Introductions to Mormon Thought

Edited by Matthew Bowman
and Joseph Spencer

EUGENE ENGLAND

A Mormon Liberal

KRISTINE L. HAGLUND

UNIVERSITY OF
ILLINOIS PRESS
Urbana, Chicago, and Springfield

Library of Congress Cataloging-in-Publication
    DataNames: Haglund, Kristine, author.
Title: Eugene England: a Mormon liberal / Kristine L
    Haglund.
Other titles: Introductions to Mormon thought.
Description: Urbana: University of Illinois Press,
    [2021] | Series: Introductions to Mormon thought
    | Includes bibliographical references and index.
Identifiers: LCCN 2021023224 (print) | LCCN
    2021023225 (ebook) | ISBN 9780252043932
    (cloth) | ISBN 9780252086007 (paperback) | ISBN
    9780252052866 (ebook)
Subjects: LCSH: England, Eugene. | Mormon
    intellectuals—Biography. | Mormon authors—
    Biography. | LCGFT: Biographies.
Classification: LCC BX8695.E54 H34 2021 (print) | LCC
    BX8695.E54 (ebook) | DDC 289.3092 [B]—dc23
LC record available at https://lccn.loc.gov/2021023224
LC ebook record available at https://lccn.loc.gov/
    2021023225

Contents

Foreword to the Introductions to Mormon Thought Series

Our purpose in this series is to provide readers with short and accessible introductions to important figures in the intellectual life of the religious movement that traces its origins to the prophetic career of Joseph Smith Jr. With an eye to the many branches of that movement (rather than solely to its largest branch, the Church of Jesus Christ of Latter-day Saints), the series features studies of what scholars have long called *Mormon* thought. We define "thought" and "intellectual life," however, quite as broadly as we define "Mormonism." We understand these terms to be inclusive, not simply of formal theological or scholarly work, but also of artistic production, devotional writing, institutional influence, political activism, and other nonscholarly pursuits. In short, volumes in the series assess the contributions of men and women who have shaped how those called Mormons in various traditions think about what "Mormonism" is.

We hope that this series marks something of a coming of age of scholarship on this religious tradition. For many years, Mormon studies have focused primarily on historical questions largely of internal interest to the (specifically) Latter-day Saint community. Such historical work has also mainly addressed the nineteenth century. Scholars have accordingly established the key sources for the study of Mormon history and culture, and they have established a broad consensus on many issues surrounding the origins and character of the religious movement. Recent work, however, has pushed academics into the work of comparison, asking larger questions in two key ways. First, recent scholars have approached these topics from a greater variety of disciplines. There has emerged in Mormon studies, in other words, increasing visibility for the disciplines of philosophy, sociology, literary criticism, and media studies, among others. Second, scholars work-ing this field have also begun to consider new topics of study—in particu-lar gender and sexuality, the status of international Mormonism, and the experience of minority groups within the tradition. We believe the field has thus reached the point where the sort of syntheses these books offer is both possible and needed.

Given these commitments, Kristine Haglund's study of Eugene Eng-land is a worthy inaugural volume to this series. England was among the most prominent of Latter-day Saint intellectuals of the twentieth century, a scholar of English literature, a personal essayist, and an institution-builder. Haglund, former editor of *Dialogue: A Journal of Mormon Thought* (the academic journal England himself founded), is similarly significant in the twenty-first century. The two make an ideal pairing of author and subject. For Haglund, England represents the pinnacle of liberal Mormon thought, a strain that flourished in the early twentieth century under the influence of the American university system. In England, it survived as a powerful alternative to the orthodox conservatism that flourished after the mid-twentieth century. Haglund links England to the contemporary American literary and philosophical scene from which he emerged, and treats him as both a literary and a historical figure. Her interdisciplinary study of England's life and thought is a tribute to the man's influence, and we are proud to offer it as the first volume of Introductions to Mormon Thought.

Matthew Bowman
Joseph Spencer

EUGENE ENGLAND

CHAPTER 1

Eugene England

A Life

Prologue: 1933

Eugene England was born in 1933, both ahead of his time, and having just missed it. He was ahead of his time, because his emphasis on the pragmatic goodness of Mormonism and the possibility of mustering Mormon theological resources in the service of progressive politics might appeal to many contemporary young Mormons, and because the kind of openness and dialogue that he hoped and worked for has subtly influenced the church's bureaucracy. He also missed his time; he might have been more at home in the early twentieth-century Mormonism that was shaped by progressive intellectuals like James E. Talmage and B. H. Roberts, who both died in the year he was born. The expansive version of Mormonism that appealed to England was being eclipsed even before he began to articulate it for his own generation of Latter-day Saints.

England had a childhood typical of Mormons in the first part of the twentieth century, and his life unfolded in a pattern that paralleled changes in Mormon life: he left the Mormon homeland in the intermountain West for missionary service, education, military service, and professional opportunities, then returned, bringing new ideas and working to assimilate them into the faith of his youth. He became an influential teacher at Brigham Young University and a champion of Mormon literature. His writings, especially his personal essays, influenced a generation of thoughtful Mormons and the academic and literary journal he cofounded, *Dialogue: A Journal of Mormon Thought*, has been a forum for and a record of Mormon intellectuals' grappling with the questions that the encounter with secular modernity pressed upon Mormons in the latter half of the twentieth century. England's life and thought are intriguing not only in their own right, but also for what they show about the contours of twentieth-century Mormonism.

As he confronted the issues of his time, England pulled at various threads from the homespun cloth of Mormonism's complex and sometimes self-contradictory doctrine. Questions about the nature of God, the status of scripture, the relative power of authoritative discourse and personal conscience, the comparative epistemological weight of science and faith, and the role of religious belief in the public sphere were all questions that England tried to address *in Mormon terms*, even when his answers put him at odds with church authorities and other believers. But he also imported terminology from American cultural and political discourse to discussions of church doctrine and ecclesiology. This, too, is quintessentially Mormon—the collapse of social, political, and ecclesiastical worlds has been a frequently criticized and occasionally celebrated feature of Mormonism.

In a speech to the English Department faculty at BYU near the end of his life, England began by mentioning two formative experiences that had convinced him of the reality of Jesus Christ's saving mission and of the divine authority of the leaders of the Church of Jesus Christ of Latter-day Saints. The result of those experiences, he said, was that he became both liberal and conservative. His conviction of and devotion to Jesus opened his mind and heart to causes he categorized as "liberal"—"equal consumption of world resources, justice for minority or dispossessed peoples, opposition to all wars." His certainty about the divine authority vested in Mormon prophets and apostles made him "conservative," he said, although his definition of "conservative" might not have been what his audience expected: "a firm, conservative confidence in the church and its leaders as well as the gospel, such that I have never felt any need to avoid difficult issues or to simply accept culturally prescribed boundaries. I have felt able to explore our history without fear, to examine troubling questions of doctrine and Church practice, to face squarely the humanness of our leaders."[1]

He was conservative in cultural ways, too. He enlisted in the ROTC and spent several years in the air force; he married young and was devoted to his wife and six children; he was registered as a Republican for most of his life; and he was a devout and actively practicing member of the LDS Church for his entire life. But, during his life and after his death, almost everyone has described him as a "liberal Mormon." In part, this has to do with the way that American religions aligned themselves politically in the 1970s and 1980s, so that England's political engagement in secular liberal causes was the most salient identifier for other Mormons. But Mormon usage of "conservative" and "liberal" means something in religious terms that doesn't neatly map onto American political or theological categories, and Eugene England's life was lived at the temporal and geographical center of the widening cultural divide.

Theologically, of course, there has never been any such thing as a Mormon liberal, at least not in the ways that most scholars of Christianity have applied the term. Talmage and Roberts were "liberal" in a quite narrow sense that had more to do with a general openness to modernity and an approach to religion that valorized the human capacity for reason in understanding the things of God rather than with the kinds of scriptural criticism and the historicized Jesus that came to be called "liberal" in other Christian denominations.[2]

Mormonism has no doctrine of inerrancy, and indeed allows an open canon, with three books of scripture in addition to the Bible as the "Standard Works," and yet most lay Mormon discourse is grounded in a quite literalist scriptural hermeneutic. There is no Mormon doctrine of infallibility, and yet in practice, extreme deference is accorded to authoritative pronouncements, especially those from the highest level of the church hierarchy (the First Presidency and the Quorum of the Twelve Apostles), but even to the opinions of local lay leaders. Most importantly, Mormonism has no real mechanism for authorizing a unitary theological interpretation, and no seminaries or training programs for its mostly lay clergy, so that what is considered "authoritative" doctrine varies widely, and Mormons with significantly divergent beliefs may consider themselves perfectly orthodox. Moreover, Mormon scripture valorizes individual intellectual effort as salvific: "if a person acquires more knowledge and intelligence in this life through his diligence and obedience than another, he will have so much the advantage in the world to come."[3] Early Mormonism was optimistic about scientific progress, and regarded scientific discovery as similar to religious revelation as a means for human beings to come to understand the mind of God.

This emphasis on personal intellectual striving corresponded, perhaps surprisingly, with a consistently conservative ecclesiology characterized by a strong centralized authority. Mormons endured serious conflict with their

Eugene England

American neighbors and government in the nineteenth century, and this conflict was often initiated or intensified by dissent from within. Thus loyalty and unity became primary organizational and psychological values, if not theological ones. In the Mormon struggle to belong in America, there were never clear demarcations between religious, ideological, and political strife; institutional hypervigilance could trigger fiercely defensive reactions over apparently minor disagreements. And because there was no ecclesiastical mechanism for adjudicating the fundamental theological questions at issue, doctrinal conflict became personalized—occasionally there were ecclesiastical sanctions for dissenters within the church, but more often, disputes over the authority to pronounce doctrine played out in ad hoc silencing or ostracization of people who taught controversial ideas like evolution or higher criticism. However, their ideas were often not officially repudiated, and so the next generation confronted the most difficult questions again, and different ideas dominated different eras. Besides Roberts's and Talmage's deaths, the year of England's birth marks the beginning of J. Reuben Clark's ascent through the central church hierarchy. Clark, an attorney and civil servant with a forceful personality, conservative politics, and religious views that tended toward fundamentalism, was called as a counselor to President Heber J. Grant in 1933. He was ordained an apostle a year later, and over the nearly three decades he served, the Quorum increasingly comprised men like Joseph Fielding Smith Jr., Ezra Taft Benson, Mark E. Peterson, and Harold B. Lee, who had more absolutist views of God, more literalist views about scripture, and less friendly attitudes toward science than their predecessors like Roberts, Talmage, and John A. Widtsoe.

Eugene England's life and work tell us a great deal about the ways Mormonism evolved in the mid- to late twentieth century because he cherished and championed an optimistic Mormonism that was open to liberalizing ideas from American culture, at the same time as he remained devoted to an institutional Mormonism that was gradually narrowing the range of acceptable beliefs in an attempt to streamline doctrine for a globally expanding church. The simultaneous fact of his twinned, sometimes opposing commitments—to his interpretation of Mormon doctrines that impelled him toward political and cultural liberalism, and to the conservative church that he loved and saw as a vehicle for progress, even when it moved haltingly—was the challenging and enlivening tension of his life and thought.

Safe Valleys

George Eugene England Jr. was born on 22 July 1933 in Logan, Utah. His parents, Dora Rose Hartvigsen England and George Eugene England, owned a farm in Downey, Idaho, where George Jr.—always known as Eugene or Gene—spent much of his childhood. England's recollections of the farm and surrounding valley are idyllic, and suggest his poetic sensibility:

> I grew up in a safe valley. The years five through twelve, when we are most sensuously attached to the landscape and when, I think, the foundations of identity are firmly laid I lived in gardens and wheatfields.
>
> ... My heart yearned, on early May mornings, when the brisk southern Idaho wind still moved the tops of sagebrush along our fencelines. ... There would be one or two mild yellow buttercups ... and by late May a few wild honeysuckles, the blossoms washed pink and detachable, made to be plucked off delicately and delicately set between the lips so the tube under the blossom could be sucked for the smallest, most delicate taste, deep on the tongue.[4]

In England's mind, the landscape became deeply intertwined with his love of his family and his Mormon faith. One of the formative experiences he often returned to in his writing happened on the farm, when he had gone with his father to weed some fallow ground and attend to the growing wheat. In the speech to the BYU faculty mentioned above, he describes his father praying over the grain:

> We kept our feet between the rows as we walked out on a ridge, I just learning how to imitate his motion of plucking a stalk to examine critically its forming kernels. He asked me to kneel with him, and he spoke, I thought to Christ, about the wheat. He pledged again, as I had heard him at home, to give all the crop, all beyond our bare needs, to build the kingdom, and he claimed protection from drought and hail and wind. I felt, beside and in me, something, a person, it seemed, something more real than the wheat or the ridge or the sun, something warm like the sun but warm inside my head and chest and bones, someone like us but strange, thrilling, fearful but safe.[5]

This account seems quintessentially Mormon—the intertwining of the spiritual and material worlds, the ideal of consecrating one's surplus to the community and church (which were mostly the same thing in small towns in the Mormon corridor in those years), and the embodied metaphysics of a God who promises to make truth known by "caus[ing] that your bosom shall burn within you." In several of his essays, England mentions measuring other ideas and intuitions by comparison to this earliest transcendent experience. He does not seem to have developed or indulged skepticism about this epistemology. It is one of the things that most deeply marks him as Mormon.

Another episode that figures in many of England's own accounts of his spiritual formation was a visit by an apostle to a church meeting England attended when he was twelve.

> In those days, [stake conferences] were held every three months and included at least two, two-hour sessions on Sunday. The most interesting highlights to us children were the quavery songs literally "rendered" by the "Singing Mothers" and the sober sustaining of the stake No Liquor–Tobacco Committee.
>
> But one conference was particularly memorable. I was twelve and sitting near the front because my father was being sustained as a high councilor in a newly formed stake. I had just turned around in my seat to tease my sister, who was sitting behind me, when I felt something, vaguely familiar, burning at the center of my heart and bones and then almost physically turning me around to look at the transfigured face of Apostle Harold B. Lee, the "visiting authority." He had suddenly interrupted his prepared sermon and was giving the new stake an apostolic blessing. And I became aware, for a second and confirming time in my life, of the presence of the Holy Ghost and the special witness of Jesus Christ. How many boring stake conferences would I attend to be even once in the presence of such grace? Thousands—all there are. That pearl is without price.[6]

As the experience with his father in the wheatfield had convinced England of the reality of Jesus and the possibility of personal communion with the divine, this later experience with a visiting church authority affirmed to him that participation in the institutional church and respect—even reverence—for its leaders was also an avenue of access to divinity. The first experience hearkened back to the agrarian, communitarian Mormonism of early Utah; the second pointed toward the emphasis on church leaders' authority and divine commission that would become more and more important as the church expanded and faced the challenges of governing a global faith.

Early religious experiences seem not to have curtailed youthful mischief-making. His friend Bert Wilson remembered that England was smart, but mischievous. "Eugene got straight A's in every subject except behavior, comportment. He got a D in that one. . . . He was just a smart-alecky kid at times. He would say things and do things, just like typical sixth graders do when they misbehave. But, at that same time, I got all A's, too, and I got a C in comportment. I wasn't as bad as Eugene was."[7] The family moved to Salt Lake City when Gene was a young teen, but continued to work the farm through Gene's high school years, so he spent many summers working there. By then, England's mischief-making was being overtaken by more earnest and bookish pursuits. Wilson's remembrance continues: "We spent a lot of time together while I was working at the [grain] elevator and during the summers when he would come back. We would share books, trade books. We started talking about books and issues of the day, much more than other kids did, I think. We didn't read, necessarily, the world's greatest literature. . . . But we talked and we shared."[8] Like many other friends, Wilson also recalled that England always tried to engage people in conversation, that he didn't shy away from controversy, and wanted to get all sides of the story.

Another friend from high school in Salt Lake was impressed by Gene's seriousness: "I also confess to having thought of Gene as maybe never having been a little boy. It seemed like he popped into the world like a few pop into the world, grown up without having to grow. He just seemed to be serious and mature and dependable, responsible. Always."[9]

This penchant for serious conversation comes up again and again in the reminiscences of friends. Jim McMichael, a friend from graduate school at Stanford, describes the quality of his conversations with Gene in reverential terms: "It's hard for me to sort out what else it was about him besides his patience and his seriousness and his intelligence and his sensibility; what else it was about him that made our conversations as good as they were. It just worked, and in a way that I hadn't experienced to that point in my life with anybody. It was just uncommon. I treasured every bit of it. I looked forward to the next conversation."[10]

Wasatch Foothills to Western Samoa

Both the need and the talent for serious dialogue seem to have been deeply embedded in England's personality. Another high school friend recalled that England and three close friends organized study groups to talk about gospel topics on Sunday evenings, and that they sometimes brought their dates home quite late from those conversations. Among the friends who participated in those groups was Charlotte Hawkins, who lived a few blocks from the England family. Although they were not in the same ward, they were in the same stake (a group of congregations roughly analogous to a diocese). Gene's mother had met Charlotte and, according to his friend Floyd Astin, "his mother told Gene that he ought to get to know her as she was very pretty and his mother was very impressed with her."[11] However, Charlotte dated Floyd through much of high school, so, although they spent a lot of time together in a close-knit group of friends, Gene and Charlotte did not begin dating until they were both students at the University of Utah.[12] Their first date together was the "Hello Dance" for freshmen in 1952. They married a year later, in December 1953.

At the University of Utah, England majored in mathematics and was a member of the LDS fraternity Lambda Delta Sigma. One of his favorite and most influential teachers was Lowell Bennion, with whom England took religion courses at the LDS Institute.[13] England admired Bennion, and was deeply influenced by his thought and his life. England became interested in pedagogy from observing the differences between Bennion's classes and the instruction typical in LDS Sunday Schools. He was particularly impressed by Bennion's use of Socratic questioning to guide discussion and elicit reasoning rather than impose learning. He also appreciated Bennion's tripartite religious epistemology—Bennion taught that religious ideas should be evaluated not only with respect to the authority of those who presented them, or in response to their emotional resonance, but also by their congruence with reason, experience, and the fundamental tenets previously revealed in scripture and prophetic teachings. Bennion's methods impressed England, and Bennion's example of active service and involvement in humanitarian causes influenced England's thought and aspirations. In an appreciation composed for Bennion's eightieth birthday, England wrote that "All over the world there are former students and colleagues in business offices and classrooms and kitchens and slums, who go about doing good to 'the least of these' Christ's brothers and sisters, because of the teaching and example of Lowell Bennion."[14] Although England's engagement was often more overtly political than Bennion's, his teacher's example of thoughtful, contemplative faith joined with vigorous Christian service had a profound impact on the way he thought and the way he spent his time throughout his life.[15]

Bennion's teaching also connected England to the progressive Mormonism of the early twentieth century. Bennion emphasized the life of the mind as an element of religion, as well as the importance of a religious community grounded in rational principles: "Religion must be more than feeling, more than even faith and good will. The life of man, living in society, needs to be understood. There are factual and rational aspects to the economic, political, and social life of man. To have any impact on these, we must understand both the nature of society and gospel principles."[16] Bennion appreciated and taught a version of Mormonism that emphasized the importance of education as a religious duty and learning as a joyful expression of human beings' eternal intelligence:

> Man is not simply God's creature. . . . There is something in man that is co-eternal with the Creator himself. . . . It seems clear that the intelligent basis of man's life, including his capacity for creative and moral living, is uncreated, and co-eternal with God and with other aspects of the universe. If so, man's relationship with Deity, with his fellow intelligences, and with himself has been, is, and ever will be creative and dynamic.[17]

It is notable that Bennion, who had written Sunday School manuals and other official church curriculum and been an influential teacher in the Church Educational System for decades, fell into disfavor with church authorities in the later years of his life and was relieved of his teaching duties and marginalized within CES.[18] The theological trends that shadowed the latter part of Bennion's career would also shadow England's work at church-sponsored Brigham Young University.

England intended to serve a full-time mission for the church, but since the number of missionaries who could serve was limited by Korean War draft policies, he was encouraged by a church leader to marry instead. He and Charlotte were then called to serve a mission together in Samoa less than a year after their marriage. A brief memoir, "Mission to Paradise," published in 1999, recounts many experiences typical of LDS missionary reminiscences—descriptions of exotic foods (the liquid from green coconuts, which tasted "like almonds, a little like ginger ale, like nothing else") and customs (a kava ceremony to honor visiting church president David O. McKay), fortuitous encounters with eager gospel learners, and miraculous faith healing.[19]

"Mission to Paradise" also includes some reflections that might not be common in the journals of young missionaries—England notes, for instance, that he and Charlotte had taken an anthropology class together at the University of Utah, where they had read Margaret Mead, and learned to recognize the kinds of cultural imperialism to which missionaries were susceptible. While seeing his own temptations to racism and classism, England felt that the values they were teaching were truly helpful to Samoans who converted. He mentions in particular that insisting on formal, legal marriages as a requirement for LDS baptism "did in fact make for more loving and nurturing relationships between the couple and with their children."[20]

England had begun college as a math major, and had joined the ROTC. However, he enjoyed his English classes and liked to write. After returning from Samoa, he especially enjoyed his English classes with Jack Adamson. Adamson had, like England, grown up in Idaho, and been raised Mormon. He served a mission to Scotland, but later became disaffected from Mormonism. However, he remained interested both in Mormonism and in religion generally, teaching classes on the Bible as literature. He was a skillful and dedicated teacher, and his classes influenced England's eventual decision to major in English. Like England, Adamson was especially interested in the moral and ethical qualities of literature. His convictions about the moral dimensions of reading and studying literature were confirmed by his experience as a Fulbright Scholar in India. Adamson came to believe that considering the ethical and moral content of literature together with its esthetics yielded richer understanding than "the barren and pedantic analyses [he] had heard in American seminars." England's attunement to the ethical dimensions of literature may have been nurtured by Adamson's feeling that "to divorce the esthetic from the ethical and moral is to dissect our humanity."[21]

England graduated from the University of Utah in 1957, and went to Massachusetts Institute of Technology (MIT) for a year of meteorology training to fulfill his ROTC obligation to the air force. In Cambridge, the Englands joined a growing community of Latter-day Saint graduate students and their families, meeting in the brick chapel, which had been dedicated just the year before, across the street from Henry Wadsworth Longfellow's stately home on Brattle Street. Members of the ward included historians Richard and Claudia Bushman, the future University of Utah president Chase Peterson and his wife Grethe, historian Laurel Ulrich and her husband Gael who was studying chemical engineering at MIT, Harvard Business School student (and later professor) Gene Dalton and his wife Bonnie, Harvard Law School student Ken Handley and his wife Kate, and many others who would become influential in the Mormon intellectual world. Friends recall a close-knit group of young couples, mostly with small children, who had fun together and also made time for earnest discussion of their faith in relation to the ideas they were encountering in their studies.[22]

The Englands were part of the first significant outmigration of Latter-day Saints from Utah and the Mormon settlements in the western United States. After World War II, the number of graduates from Utah universities increased enormously. Enrollment at BYU, for instance, increased from 5,000 in 1951 to over 25,000 in 1976. During this period Latter-day Saint college graduates increasingly left Utah for graduate school or military service and, in significant numbers, settled outside of the intermountain West.

California: Victor Valley to Santa Clara Valley

After MIT, the Englands moved to George Air Force Base outside of Victorville, California. England finished his ROTC obligation to the air force working for two years as a weather officer. Jerry Cannon, who worked with England in the leadership of the Elders Quorum (one of three groups of men who comprised a typical ward at that time), remembered England's early concern with the immediate practical implications of church teachings. He described an episode when the LDS Church's policy forbidding men of African descent to be ordained to the priesthood was discussed in a Sunday School class. (The LDS Church did not allow men of African descent to be ordained to the priesthood until 1978, and various racist rationales were adduced to explain the policy.) Although England tried to counter racist comments that were made during the course of the discussion, one particularly offensive remark prompted a couple to walk out of the class and then not return to church again. Cannon recalled that he and

England had visited with this couple in their home several times before the incident occurred, and they continued to visit them,

> trying to smooth things over and encourage them to come back to church. We shared over and over how this was just one person's opinion and that the church was true even though some of the people aren't too good, or aren't great thinkers or are not too compassionate. Gene always had a real love for the people he served. . . . It was very uplifting for me to visit this family with Gene and to hear his comments and watch how he handled this situation. I know that going with Gene helped me develop a better attitude myself and was influential in how I handled things in later positions I held in the church.[23]

After completing his air force service, Gene returned briefly to Salt Lake City, then began graduate studies in English at Stanford as a Danforth Fellow. Like many campuses in those years, Stanford was being rocked by political debate and student activism. England's thoroughly Mormon response was to think and talk about what Mormonism had to say about these issues. Although he had been more politically conservative than many of his peers, and had served in the military, he became increasingly opposed to the nation's involvement in the Vietnam War. In 1964, he came to believe that the government was lying about what happened in the Gulf of Tonkin and that the war was immoral. Being convinced, he said, "that a president had lied and that our government was willing to deceive us and kill people far away, in my name and using my taxes—for what seemed more and more an unworthy and unjust cause—was a life-changing experience."[24] He joined the Graduate Student Coordinating Council, an activist group that published and distributed an antiwar newsletter, organized rallies, and tried to influence local policy discussions about things like fair housing.

At the same time, he was teaching lessons on scripture at the LDS Institute, serving in the bishopric in the Stanford Ward, and keeping busy with a family that grew to include six children. In this full life, England began to recognize that his own sense of a coherent Mormon life did not necessarily make sense either to other Mormons or to people outside of the church. He described a day when a graduate student friend said to him, "You've got to let your hair grow long, to show which side you're on," just a few hours before a church leader said, "Gene, you've got to keep your hair short . . . to show you're really OK despite your liberal ideas."[25] England's distaste for cultural shibboleths would persist throughout his life, as would the discomfort of friends and church leaders who wanted clear signals about which side he was on.

England felt that gospel of Jesus he learned through Mormonism impelled him toward "liberal" causes—concern for the marginalized, commitment to equality for all of God's children, and pacifism. He came into conflict with leaders of his local congregation who emphasized Mormon teachings that encouraged more deference to authority, both ecclesiastical and civil. While England felt that his ideas were orthodox and grounded in scripture, those who disagreed with him also believed that they were advocating scripturally mandated doctrine. A Latter-day Saint Article of Faith (composed by Joseph Smith to explain Mormonism at a newspaper editor's request, and later canonized) asserts that "We believe in being subject to kings, presidents, rulers, and magistrates, in obeying, honoring, and sustaining the law," and this scripture often becomes warrant for silencing any sort of political dissent or even discussion among the Mormon faithful.[26] Ultimately, England was asked to stop discussing anything "political"—which included the LDS Church's prohibition of Black members receiving the priesthood—in the Institute classes he was teaching.

While England complied (mostly) with the request from his superiors to steer clear of controversy in his Institute classes, he craved discussion of the topics that occupied his own religious thinking. With several others, he began planning to launch a periodical to foster conversation and exploration beyond the official curriculum of church classes. In a later oral history, he recalled that it was an idea that had been germinating for some time:

> It was during my undergraduate years that I really started thinking about a journal of this kind. . . . [My] concerns focused in two areas: one that became increasingly important to me was the need for people with intellectual gifts of various kinds to feel at home in the Church or to feel there was some kind of community in the Church in which to express themselves. Along with this kind of religious interest, I found myself not too pleased with the cultural level of the Church magazines, the quality of writing and editing I saw there.[27]

England first met with Frances Menlove, Paul Salisbury, and Wesley Johnson early in 1965, and by spring of 1966, they had published the first issue of *Dialogue: A Journal of Mormon Thought*. (See chapter 3 for a fuller discussion of the journal and its impact.)

At one remove from concerns about the Vietnam War and other pressing social issues, England began a dissertation on the poet Frederick Tuckerman, a reclusive contemporary of Emily Dickinson and Ralph Waldo Emerson. Tuckerman's work had been obscure during his lifetime, but had had a few twentieth-century champions, notably Edmund Wilson, whose work on Civil War poetry had briefly revived interest in the reclusive poet. England later wrote to his friend, church General Authority Marion D. Hanks, that Tuckerman's work was as good as Emily Dickinson's and would cause a reevaluation of American Transcendentalism (a prophecy that has not yet come to pass).[28]

Minnesota Prairie and Utah Valley

In 1970, Ron Lee, who had been a Danforth Fellow at Stanford with England, and had gone to teach at St. Olaf College in Minnesota, contacted him to see if he would be interested in a position as dean of academic affairs at St. Olaf. England accepted readily, and moved with Charlotte and their children to Northfield at the start of the 1970–71 academic year. The college was expanding its student body from 2,500 to 3,000, and undergoing what consultants would now call a "Visioning Exercise"—evaluating current programs and setting directions for the future. England was influential in setting up a Subcommittee on Teaching and Learning, incorporating new teaching techniques and a focus on values in teaching. England also established a lecture series on "A Teacher's Faith and Values," which led to the publication of a collection of essays with the same title.

During the time he was at St. Olaf, he was called as branch president (pastor) of the tiny Faribault, Minnesota, Branch, a congregation of about twenty families in and around Northfield. In the structure of Latter-day Saint Churches, average-sized congregations are called "wards," while smaller congregations in areas where the church is less established are called "branches." These small congregations tend to be close-knit, often with just a few families doing most of the work that is spread among many hands in larger congregations. England's experiences ministering to that congregation were transformative; many years later, his recollections of that branch were the source material for his best-known essay, *Why the*

Church Is as True as the Gospel. After England's death, branch members Ray and Jeanne Jacobsen described the intimate social and spiritual bonds that connected them:

> Nearby the England place was a brook with small trout that could be seen, also cows grazing in the nearby pastures . . . a bucolic atmosphere that we, living in town, could enjoy and especially find as a retreat. Many family picnics are well remembered in this atmosphere, as are baptisms held in the prepared deeper section of the slow-moving stream, where many would remember their unique feeling in stepping into a "first" kind of spiritual relationship. These memories are treasured as a time when our families were innocent, unknowing of their life ahead when they would face their individual choices and challenges.[29]

In 1975, having been denied tenure at St. Olaf, England returned with his family to Salt Lake City. He taught at the LDS Institute of Religion at the University of Utah and worked in the Church Historian's Office, conducting research on Brigham Young, which eventually yielded the biography *Brother Brigham*.[30] While Mormon intellectuals have been occasionally prone to think of Joseph Smith as Mormonism's earliest thinker, and Brigham Young as mostly a skilled "doer," this study left England with a lasting admiration for Young's thought as well as his work. England noted that Young had always claimed to teach only what he had learned from Joseph Smith, and suggested that "the Lord may have preserved Brigham Young for thirty-three years after Joseph's death partly to . . . preserve, through his sermons, the full legacy of Joseph's mind. Those sermons are our major source, however neglected, for understanding Mormon thought, especially in its practical, historical context. It is there we can find the roots of modern Mormonism."[31] In particular, England credited Brigham Young with elaborating on and teaching Joseph Smith's "eternalism" and "naturalism," that is, his vision of existence consisting of physical elements and natural laws, without beginning or end. He also credits Brigham Young with fully developing the notion of "eternal progression"—the idea that human beings can continue to learn, progress, and create forever, growing into beings with godlike knowledge, wisdom, and power. England also found in Brigham Young's sermons and writings the valorization of struggle and paradox that would become central to England's own thinking: "that increase is only possible through a struggle with opposition toward higher states of enlightenment and organization—or lawful, creative control of self and environment. Knowledge is the key to this power to increase, to create further life, and the essential knowledge is dialectical, or knowledge of opposites."[32]

In 1977, England accepted a position in the English Department at the university named for Brigham Young. From 1979 to 1983, he taught in the Freshman Honors Colloquium—an interdisciplinary seminar that allowed students and professors to work together across disciplinary boundaries to synthesize knowledge from a variety of perspectives. England often spoke of how much he enjoyed the freedom to include spiritual and religious perspectives in discussions of history, literature, and science. Both as a Danforth Fellow at Stanford and in his role at St. Olaf College, England had thought carefully about pedagogical issues and methods, and he brought those ideas into the classroom at BYU. In his first speech to the faculty of the College of Humanities in 1978, England described the issues other universities were facing in designing a general education curriculum that would give direction to the undergraduate education they offered, and lamented the trend toward hyperspecialization. He offered the model they were working on in the honors program at BYU as an example of how one might design a curriculum that would be truly interdisciplinary and also intellectually coherent:

> Three faculty, a graduate assistant and 70 students are engaged in a year-long, eight credit-hours per term, study of "Romanticism," both as a recurring dimension of human understanding and as a particular watershed in history which formed (for better or worse) the foundations of modern thought. We are concerned with matters as diverse as the transition in human attempts to understand the physical universe that occur from Galileo to Newton to Einstein and the response of Wordsworth and Keats to the mechanistic universe that they perceived in Newton, who for them had "unwoven the rainbow."
>
> . . . They have had to learn fundamental modes of scientific thinking and teach them to each other. In one of our most successful experiments, we helped them learn the concept of entropy and think it through not only in terms of basic heat loss in the universe but [in] such apparently unrelated issues as deterioration of order in information processing and some of the implications for the nature of God, theories of evolution, and the doctrine of resurrection. We taught them calculus . . . in terms

of fundamental concepts such as instantaneous rate of change and way of thinking which enabled them to respond to the claim that the invention of the calculus by Newton was as great an act of human imagination as the plays of Shakespeare.[33]

England also taught specialized courses in Shakespeare and led the BYU study abroad program in London. With professor and playwright Tim Slover, he designed an intensive two-month London Theatre study abroad program that would be affordable and accessible to more students than the full semester program. Slover recalled that England's critical method was deeply personal; his aesthetic sense required that good art should be moral—that it should reflect the moral consciousness of the author, and that its effect on its audience should require moral judgment and evoke moral action. England's belief that good artists must also *be* good caused trouble for him when he taught plays like *The Merchant of Venice* and *The Taming of the Shrew*. Those plays use imagery and language that reflect the anti-Semitism and sexism of Shakespeare's age, and yet England resisted the characterization of Shakespeare himself as sexist or anti-Semitic. "This attribution," Slover recalled, "actually caused Gene physical pain. And so, because the Bard he knew was neither racist nor sexist, he spent much effort in the classroom, on buses, in restaurants—once with me in a public bathroom—expounding his theories that exculpated Shakespeare from the opprobrium."[34]

Students and colleagues remember England as extraordinarily generous and kind, going out of his way to attend to them as whole human beings, both inside and outside of the classroom. In this Charlotte was a full partner and colleague, constantly opening their home, baking bread and making ice cream that many describe as sacramental.

Early in his BYU career, however, a significant conflict arose between England and Joseph Fielding McConkie, a professor of religion. Because McConkie was the son of LDS apostle Bruce McConkie (a member of one of the highest governing bodies of the Church of Jesus Christ of Latter-day Saints), the controversy drew more attention and had weightier consequences than most faculty disagreements. The immediate point of controversy was theological, perhaps somewhat abstract and arcane; however, the questions over which England and McConkie disagreed turn out to be foundational to England's thinking and writing, and will be examined in detail in chapter 3.

At the heart of the dispute was a disagreement over the nature of God—England favored the idea that God can progress. The central thesis of his talk was simply that students at the university were undertaking a godly endeavor, that learning would help them both understand and imitate God's work.

McConkie read an advance copy of England's speech, and called England to warn him that his ideas would displease his father. England invited Joseph McConkie to make a public response to the lecture; McConkie's rebuttal was a harsh critique that bordered on personal rebuke. Several months later, Bruce McConkie delivered a devotional address at BYU in which he declared that the idea that God is progressing was one of "Seven Deadly Heresies." England and the elder McConkie exchanged several letters about the issue, with the final result that England did not speak again publicly about the question of God's possible progression until after McConkie's death.

His conflict with Bruce McConkie was not the end of England's involvement with controversy at BYU. After his experience in the Graduate Student Coordinating Council at Stanford, England remained politically active throughout his life. During his time at BYU, he was involved in antiwar protests, antinuclear actions, feminist activism, and working for greater academic freedom at BYU. Unlike Stanford or St. Olaf's, BYU was not accustomed to political activism from either faculty or students. BYU had weathered the upheaval of the 1960s with hardly any student protests, but in the late 1980s and 1990s, BYU experienced small protests, mostly over issues related to academic freedom and feminism. England found himself more and more in conflict with the administration, along with other members of the English Department. In 1992, English professors Gail Houston and Cecilia Farr were denied continuing status (BYU's version of tenure). Farr was fired, nominally for poor scholarship, despite having published more than many candidates for tenure in the department. The inciting incident for her firing was a speech she had given at a pro-choice rally in Salt Lake City (and the subsequent publication of the text), in which she declared that she was personally opposed to abortion but believed that pregnant women should have a legal right to self-determination. Like Farr, Houston taught feminist approaches to literature. Moreover, she had made a passing reference to a prayer in which she sought guidance from "heavenly parents," which one student had complained about to a member of the board of trustees.

(While Mormon doctrine posits the existence of a Heavenly Mother, she is little discussed, and President Gordon B. Hinckley had admonished in a 1991 General Conference address that "in light of the instruction we have received from the Lord Himself, I regard it as inappropriate for anyone in the Church to pray to our Mother in Heaven."[35]) Ultimately, Houston was denied tenure and left BYU in 1996.[36] In 1995, another English Department faculty member, writer Brian Evenson, was drawn into conflict with the BYU administration over concerns about violence portrayed in a work of fiction he had published; he also left the university.

England's involvement in these cases was mostly indirect. However, he wrote some pieces for the *Student Review* (an independent campus newspaper) whose headlines made it clear where his sympathies lay: "Let's Renounce the Remaining Racism,"[37] "Prior Restraint and Guilt by Association: Reflections on Academic Freedom at BYU,"[38] "Combatting Racism and Sexism at BYU: An Open Letter to Faculty and Students."[39] England took issue particularly with statements by Apostles Dallin H. Oaks (who had been the president of BYU from 1971 to 1980) and Russell M. Nelson, which condemned participation in publications or forums that allowed "alternate voices," and suggested that "surely a stalwart would not lend his or her good name to periodicals, programs, or forums that feature offenders who do sow 'discord among brethren' (Prov. 6:19)."[40] In August 1992, England's frustration boiled over in the question-and-answer session of a presentation at the Sunstone Symposium (an annual gathering sponsored by *Sunstone* magazine as an open forum for presentations and discussions on all aspects of Mormon life—the kind of forum condemned by Nelson and Oaks). England spoke out in condemnation of the ominously named "Strengthening the Church Membership Committee," a group formed by the central church administration in Salt Lake City to monitor publications and news coverage of dissenting intellectuals. His denunciation was picked up by a TV camera and reported in the national news, much to England's chagrin.

In this atmosphere of increasing tension between scholars, activists, and church leaders, in May of 1993, Boyd K. Packer gave a talk to a group of church leaders, in which he described the three most pressing dangers to the church: "There are three areas where members of the Church, influenced by social and political unrest, are being caught up and led away. I chose these three because they have made major invasions into the membership of the Church. . . . The dangers I speak of come from the gay-lesbian movement, the feminist movement (both of which are relatively new), and the ever-present challenge from the so-called scholars or intellectuals."[41]

Later that year, six intellectuals, several of whom had published their controversial work in *Dialogue*, the journal that England had founded, were subjected to church discipline. Four were excommunicated, and two more were "disfellowshipped" (a punishment that stops short of removing the member from the church, but prohibits him or her from participating in sacraments and lay ministry). England's response was an essay titled "On Spectral Evidence," in which he took Arthur Miller's treatment of the Salem witch trials in *The Crucible* as a text, and inveighed against the use of "spectral evidence," caricatures, and partial understanding of the other to label and condemn.

He specifically decried the ways that the labels "conservative" and "liberal" were being used among Mormons to draw lines and choose sides, a theme he would return to repeatedly in the later years of his life:

> What has happened to the terms "liberal" and "conservative" in recent years is a primary example of the serious mischief that reliance on spectral evidence can do to a community. Those terms traditionally were simply political labels . . . ; they stood for the two main different, but honorable, positions from which people could seek to improve society. . . . But in the last dozen years, especially the right wing of my own party, the Republicans, have tried to make those labels, those mere specters which before were only simple and rough guides to political tendencies, stand for the whole identity of persons as good (conservatives) or evil (liberals).[42]

England's peacemaking efforts continued through the next year, when he wrote privately to Apostle Neal Maxwell, proposing the creation of a forum where church leaders and scholars, artists, and others involved in the Mormon "independent sector" could meet to discuss issues dividing church membership. In 1997, in the speech cited above, in which he described himself as both conservative and liberal, England made an impassioned plea to the English Department to try to heal the breach that had developed between factions of the faculty. He argued that they were dividing themselves into factions over issues that were ultimately insignificant, and that instead they should embrace and learn from their differences.[43]

This attempt at peacemaking and England's characteristic hope for dialogue failed, at least in the short term. A few months later, BYU President Merrill Bateman requested that England retire from the university. England left at the end of the Spring 1998 term, and accepted a position as writer in residence at Utah Valley State College (now Utah Valley University), where he set about creating a course in Mormon literature, exploring the possibility of creating a Mormon Cultural Studies program, and organizing a study abroad program centered on theater in London. He did not speak publicly about the conditions of his departure from BYU, although he later wrote of his anguish in private letters, suggesting that he had never been given an honest reason for Bateman's demand for his resignation, and in particular, that the degree to which members of the Quorum of the Twelve were involved in the decision to ask him to leave had been a subject of obfuscation. One of his colleagues at UVSC wrote that he had "never met a person who was more misunderstood or under-appreciated by his own people."[44]

Valley of the Shadow

England's extraordinary optimism and energy seemed to wane beginning around 2000. He said to colleagues that perhaps that sadness over the end of his time at BYU had caused some sort of depression. He was more explicit in a letter to Neal A. Maxwell on 16 January 2001:

> I have continued the process of self-examination and prayer for guidance and forgiveness on a daily basis—with many sleepless nights. I am worried that I may be sinking towards a serious depression and so am asking again if there is any help you can give, certainly your prayers—and anything else you think would help my repentance be more specific or efficacious. . . . If pride or rebelliousness has ever dimmed my judgment, I am profoundly sorrowful and ask your forgiveness and help in my repentance.
>
> I think I have succeeded (since your suggestion of a "course correction" [in 1995]) in my efforts to speak and write without speculation and without criticism of any of the Brethren, and that my writing over the past few years has become especially effective in building faith and sustaining the kingdom.[45]

Maxwell wrote back on 25 January. While he firmly insisted that it would be unproductive to discuss the events surrounding England's departure from

BYU, he wrote, "I want to be helpful as a friend in your search for peace of soul. If talking at this spiritual level would be of interest to you, then a meeting could surely be arranged."[46]

Before a meeting could be arranged, England collapsed, and emergency brain surgery revealed several cysts and malignant tumors. He died on 17 August 2001.

England's retirement and his death marked the end of an era in Mormon intellectual life; he was the last Mormon liberal. He was certainly not the last Latter-day Saint to be drawn to progressive social or political causes, or to wrestle with the dilemmas of authority and obedience presented to individuals in a church that makes strong demands for loyal orthodoxy. But by the time of England's death, it was no longer possible to believe, as England did, that his ideas about the nature of God and the authority of the church were in the mainstream of Mormon belief and teaching. There are many liberal and progressive Mormons in North America now, but they must understand "liberal" as a qualifier of their Mormonism—an inevitable marker of distance from full acceptance. England's liberalism grew organically from a fully Mormon identity. It was not only or most importantly an identification with the American political left, but a kind of Mormonism—open to truth from every source, optimistic about human nature and potential, and confident of the possibility of attaining sanctifying knowledge. England understood Mormon doctrine, particularly the notion that human beings are not created by God, but eternally co-extant with God, as granting humanity a radical freedom from divine coercion. His thought is profitably set in dialogue with the work of theologians like Paul Tillich and Reinhold Niebuhr and innovative philosophers like William James, but his liberal heritage came not through his own study of these sources, but through Mormon thinkers who had been performing the work of assimilation and adaptation for generations.

Few of the next generation of Mormon scholars grew up in the "safe valleys" of England's youth—in a largely agrarian Mormon world where fathers prayed over crops and General Authorities regularly came to visit. The seamless Mormon consciousness that England retained through all of his experience of dialogue and paradox seems impossible to cultivate in the twenty-first century. Mormons have scattered, and even the tight-knit clusters of Mormon graduate students in the diaspora have grown to the point that few of those students will be able to return to BYU as professors.

Academia has changed—cutthroat competition for jobs requires specialization and the kind of publication record that precludes graduate students and junior faculty from starting journals in fields unrelated to their academic specialties. The Church of Jesus Christ of Latter-day Saints has changed, too—it has grown from a small, regional sect to a worldwide church with fifteen times as many members as it claimed when England was born, with a large cadre of middle managers and an increasingly aged Quorum of the Twelve whose energies are consumed largely by administration. While the ugliness of the 1990s conflicts between Mormon intellectuals and the church's hierarchs is fading from consciousness, it will never again be possible for an earnest Mormon with academic ambitions and liberal political inclinations to believe that her religion, her scholarship, and her activism belong integrally to Mormonism. The aspirational wholeness of England's life, fractured by the evolutionary shifts in the late twentieth-century church, points to an expansive Mormonism that might have been.

Eugene England

CHAPTER 2

Toward Integrity

Essay as Form and Method

> Theological ideas . . . are . . . an extraordinarily rich resource
> for empowering the imaginative worlds of Mormon literature.
> This resource is multiplied by the dramatic and mythically
> potent Mormon history and the ethically challenging
> opportunities and demands of service, covenant-making, and
> charismatic experience in the Mormon lay church. . . .
> From the beginning, Mormons have produced many
> of their writings, including some of their best, in forms that
> until fairly recently have been dismissively called subliterary:
> diaries, letters, hymns, sermons, histories, and personal
> essays.
>
> —Eugene England and Lavina Fielding Anderson, Introduction
> to *Tending the Garden: Essays on Mormon Literature*

Eugene England championed Mormon literature, particularly the personal essay, throughout his career. In the personal essay, he found a form in which he could integrate literary, spiritual, and political ideas. He also believed that personal essays, journals, and sermons were the forms in which the richness of lived Mormonism could be represented in its full earnestness and sincerity without being cloying. England himself rarely wrote formal or heavily theorized literary criticism; even his writing directed to academic and secular audiences is focused on the ethical and personal themes of the literature he studied.

Although England does not make it explicit, his own essays and his appreciation of the form suggest that the essay form—which allows unfettered curiosity and experimentation, explores contradictions without urgency to resolve them, and situates the author within her creation—provides an ideal correspondence with England's understanding of Mormon theology, in which God is immanent in creation, and human beings are meant to try and fail and grow toward godhood in a universe that holds opposing forces and ideas in tension to create the conditions in which godlike knowledge can be acquired. His own published essay collections—*Dialogues with Myself, Why the Church Is as True as the Gospel, Making Peace*, and *The Quality of Mercy*—aimed to "show something of the range of subject matter and approach possible in the personal essay; to give a personal version of the intellectual and cultural history of Mormonism . . . and, of course, to bear witness to the conditions of [his] own growth of mind and spirit."[1]

Integrity in the Face of Anxiety

In a 1982 essay titled simply "Enduring," England describes his search for "safe places" even within the mountain-ringed, safe valley in which his family's farm was situated. His description is idyllic, a paean to an almost mythic agrarian childhood. Even there, though, he felt the stirrings of existential terror and nausea:

> One evening there began to come moments when I could feel moving into my mind, like a physical presence, the conviction that all was quite absurd. It made no sense at all that anything should exist. Something like nausea, but deeper and frightening, would grow in my stomach and chest but also at the core of my spirit, progressing like vertigo until in desperation I must jump up or talk suddenly of trivial things to break the spell and regain balance.[2]

Later, he would recognize a kindred fear in the writings of existentialist philosophers—the essay briefly mentions Paul Tillich, and his description of that existential nausea may have been influenced by passages like these from *The Courage to Be*:

> Anxiety is the state in which a being is aware of its possible nonbeing. . . . Anxiety is finitude, experienced as one's own finitude. . . .[3]

> The pain of despair is that a being is aware of itself as unable to affirm itself because of the power of nonbeing. Consequently, it wants to surrender this awareness and its presupposition, the being which is aware. It wants to get rid of itself—and it cannot.[4]

England describes his own fear as having unique contours shaped by his Mormonism. As in Tillich's description, it is the inability to escape the self-consciousness of being that pressed in on him, and since Mormon doctrine holds that human beings have always existed as intelligences, "co-eternal" with God, England wrote, "there finally is no answer to the question of why and how I exist in my essential being. I just always have, and that is where my mind balks in horror."[5] It is a different sort of fear than the existential anxiety inflected by a more traditional Christianity, which might question why God had bothered to make human beings at all.

The essay goes on, in meandering, essaying fashion, to describe situations that awaken that dread: ministering to a mother of twins, one healthy and one with severe and inexplicable disabilities; studying the many varieties of chromosomal disorders that create babies who inevitably live short and painful lives; witnessing his mother-in-law's decline and death from pancreatic cancer; trying, in a way he knew to be inadequate, to alleviate suffering. He would like, he says, "to take refuge in the mystery that an absolute God made it all out of nothing and will make sense of it or send it back to nothing," but he is denied even that solace by his conviction that the God Joseph Smith revealed will not intervene in a universe created to expand the scope of human freedom to act, a universe that requires "opposition in all things."[6]

The ending of the essay is rhetorically and philosophically unsatisfying. England draws no conclusions, but returns to the quotidian—his work as bishop, the mission of his small humanitarian aid organization, his life with his family, his middle daughter's recovery from surgery, and his eldest daughter's new love. The piece ends as it began, with a quotation from *King Lear*: "Men must endure their going hence, as their coming hither. Ripeness is all."

England's conclusion is that doing something is better than doing nothing, that integrity requires human beings not to give into the "appalling luxury" of cynicism—the moral choice is to *try*, even in the face of the profoundest doubt. That trying, for England, meant plunging in—to action, to writing, to speaking, to teaching. It meant tolerating ambiguity and messiness, even resisting closure and completeness.

Action and the Epistemology of Integrity

Many of his essays have a similar trajectory toward an acknowledgment of unresolvable difficulty and affirmation of the duty to persist in its face.

In "Letter to a College Student," for instance, England acknowledges the kinds of disillusionment that have led his young friend to distance himself from church activity—"pettiness, narrowness, deceit, and childishness," "obnoxious piety," "commercialism, exploitation of the gullible statistics, and the self-righteous refusal to admit blunder and consider change." England notes that he sees these tendencies in himself as well as other church members, and suggests "that these problems have been present whenever the Lord's Kingdom was organized among human beings." On the other hand, England points out, there is sincerity and devotion among church members, commitment to doing what they understand to be right. He describes his experience working in a small branch of the church in Minnesota, finding that "there is closeness, communication, self-development, and moving, penetrating spiritual experience available to us through our association and service in the Church—. . . feelings and experiences crucial to our joy and progression that we just wouldn't have without the Church." He exhorts his younger correspondent to return to and continue in church activity, because the people who see flaws and failures in the institution are "the ones who must do something constructive about it, because the people who are committing the errors can't see them."[7]

In "On Finding Truth and God," England offers a philosophical grounding for this privileging of action as a means of resolving intellectual dilemmas. As in the "Letter to a College Student," England comes to the question by way of a younger person seeking his advice, in this case, advice about how to acquire more certainty about the divine origin of the Book of Mormon. His vocabulary in describing the epistemological methods he recommends is active: "active desire," "energetic yearning," "questing," "persistent." Moreover, writes England, the price of faith is "willingness to accept the responsibility that such potential life [immortality] implies." Nor, he argues, can faith be static: "For many of us much of the faith that is possible in this vale of tears . . . is made possible in part by our being energetic and persistent in such questioning."[8]

England argues that at least mild skepticism is essentially positive—"if skepticism is properly understood and used it can reinforce the need for both religion and faith." An unwillingness to blindly trust authorities, religious or scientific, has, according to England, refuted faith in reductive science, reminded us of the complexity of human nature and the law of unintended consequences, and can "lead . . . back toward the balance of humility and fearlessness we find only in true *faith*."[9]

England then uses two texts from the Book of Mormon to ground an epistemological method that can give access to truth and divinity. First, he cites 2 Nephi on the necessity of opposition: "it must needs be that there is an opposition in all things." England gives weight to the explanation that follows in the Book of Mormon, that the world must be made in this way, not only to guarantee the possibility of human agency and growth, but also to maintain the fundamental order of the universe, and even its existence.

Then he describes the "experiment" Alma suggests in Alma 32. While Alma uses the term "experiment," it is not an application of impartial scientific method. Instead, Alma's experiment proceeds if the experimenter can "exercise a particle of faith," or at least "desire to believe." It is, nakedly, what we have lately come to call "motivated reasoning." The acquisition of faith, on this model, requires action, even if the initial action is only the mental action of hoping or desiring. After that, Alma prescribes more action. Having felt the seed beginning to grow in the soul, Alma says, "if ye nourish it with much care it will get root." England amplifies the active character of this labor: "We need only have the courage to hope—to desire a living and responsive universe no matter how responsible that makes us—and the integrity to test the seed and the grit to nurture the plant, whatever increasing demands that places on us."[10]

The testing of the seed involves both intellectual rigor—questioning both absolutist, scientistic conclusions and dogmatic religious propositions—and the wager of time and effort to test religious ideas in practice. England referred often to an anecdote shared by church president David O. McKay in a General Conference address in 1968. McKay related his youthful efforts to gain a conventional Mormon "testimony"—the assurance that God had spoken through Joseph Smith. He reports that he failed in his first attempts, that despite sincere and lengthy prayer, he had not received the witness he sought. It was only after he had accepted a call to serve a mission in England and labored to help others apply the principles he hoped were true that he could say that "the spiritual manifestation for which I had prayed as a boy in my teens came as a natural sequence to the performance of duty."[11]

In this legitimation of action as a tool of religious epistemology, England anticipates scholars like James K. A. Smith, Saba Mahmood, and Talal Asad who have pointed out that it is a relatively recent development that leads contemporary (especially Western Protestant) religions to privilege the interior experience of belief over outward manifestations of spiritual discipline. Asad makes this observation in relation to the rule of Saint Benedict: "The Christian notion of . . . discipline as the force necessary for coordinating an organic whole belongs to the vocabulary of duty. It presupposes a program of learning to lead a virtuous life under the authority of law, in which everyone has his or her proper place.[12] Smith suggests that Christians ought to envision Christian education as "a formative rather than just an informative project."[13]

Unlike Asad, England does not merely *describe* this epistemological method; his writing here as elsewhere is thoroughly prescriptive. Scholarly detachment was generally not among England's many virtues, even though the engaged, active, and activist nature of his work sometimes caused him a great deal of difficulty with his employers and with his church community. This was not a matter of thoughtlessness, but a deliberate choice to prioritize the moral application of knowledge in all of his work. At St. Olaf College, for instance, he and a colleague inaugurated a lecture series called "A Teacher's Faith and Values" to discuss the ways that teachers' ethical convictions inform their teaching. At BYU, he celebrated the freedom to discuss religious belief and ethical questions in literature classes.

Unlike his favorite undergraduate English teacher at the University of Utah, Jack Adamson, who declared that he had "an aversion to political activism so strong as to be almost pathological,"[14] England was drawn to energetic political and social activism. During his time at BYU, he was involved in campus activism in support of feminist causes, academic freedom, and pacifism. After being in Vatican Square in 1981 when there was an assassination attempt on Pope John Paul II, England became very concerned about the unrest and subsequent humanitarian crisis in Poland, and started an organization called Food for Poland, which raised millions of dollars' worth of food and in-kind aid to send to Polish relief agencies.

This eagerness to *do* something is, in some ways, a quintessentially Mormon characteristic, sometimes mentioned by critics who suggest that it derives from an essentially works-based soteriology. However, England's eagerness to *do* things—he liked words like "quest" and "venture"—seems more motivated by a commitment to progress that is somewhat separate from questions of salvation. This, too, is thoroughly Mormon. An important early twentieth-century Mormon thinker and church leader, John A. Widtsoe, trained as a chemist, attempted to reconcile Mormon theology with the rational methods he learned as a scientist. In his *Rational Theology*, Widtsoe articulates the understanding that underlies England's valorization of action as well as thought:

> All God's creative works . . . were first begotten of the intelligent mind, and must represent some necessity in the Great Plan. Whatever, therefore, is brought into operation on earth for the good of man, must represent great, eternal, spiritual realities. . . . It matters little, therefore, whether man devote his life to the tilling of the soil, the making of shoes, or the writing of books, so that the work be well done. All such tasks are proper, dignified, and necessary parts of the Great Plan, and will lead man along the path of eternal progression.[15]

Further, Widtsoe's articulation of Mormon teaching makes clear that teaching and doing are of a piece, all part of the religious duty of the educated Saint: "The man who is in possession of strength, acquired by any means whatsoever, is under special obligations to the community. The strong must, somehow, attach to themselves those who are weak; and as the strong move onward, they must pull with them those who are weak. If a person possesses knowledge, he must give knowledge to others, so that all may attain great knowledge."[16]

Widtsoe studied at Harvard in the 1890s, and took a course with William James, which the course catalog described as "a study of the fundamental conceptions of natural science, with special reference to theories of evolution and materialism."[17] Years later, Widtsoe mentioned the course in a letter:

> In my student days I sat at the feet of two of the great philosophers mentioned among others by Mr. Lochner: Josiah Royce and William James. Some forty-two or forty-three years ago I took a course in cosmology from William James. That was the year that Professor James had a serious case of indigestion, and I assure you that when we were through with the class we all had the sense that the cosmos was dark, dreary, and forbidding. I am not much interested in philosophy of the old kind. I prefer to take the modern type, which builds from observed facts, both outward and inward.[18]

Whatever a dyspeptic William James may have conveyed about the cosmos, his empiricist approach to religion would certainly have been compatible with Widtsoe's notion of building "from observed facts, both outward and inward." Witdsoe had left Harvard by the time James delivered the lectures that became *The Will to Believe* so it is unlikely there is any deliberate reference to James via Widtsoe in England's insistence that religious beliefs must sometimes be acted upon in the absence of rational proofs. Still, many of James's arguments are nicely illustrated in England's best-known essay, *Why the Church Is as True as the Gospel*, which affirms the necessity of action as a means of acquiring faith. James's argument in *The Will to Believe* is that certain kinds of truths are brought about by acting *as though* one believes—a person who wonders whether a new acquaintance likes her can evoke that acquaintance's *dis*like by waiting to offer any trust or warmth until she is certain of the person's liking. The inverse is also true—if one behaves trustingly, offering the tokens of friendliness, one is far more likely to eventually be proven correct in the hypothesis of friendship. "There are . . . cases," James says, "where a fact cannot come at all unless a preliminary faith exists in its coming." Many of the cases James enumerates are communal:

> A social organism of any sort whatever . . . is what it is because each member proceeds to his own duty with a trust that the other members will simultaneously do theirs. Wherever a desired result is achieved by the co-operation of many independent persons, its existence as a fact is a pure consequence of the precursive faith in one another of those immediately concerned. A government, an army, a commercial system, a ship, a college, an athletic team all exist on this condition, without which not only is nothing achieved, but nothing is even attempted.[19]

England's essay takes as its case a social organism James leaves out of his list—a church. The essay begins with a cliché Mormons sometimes repeat, that the gospel is true, but the church is imperfect. In this, they are attempting to articulate a split between the abstract, but perfectly correct, teachings of scriptures and prophets and the imperfect attempts of human beings to put those teachings into practice. England points out the impossibility of disentangling a set of pure and internally consistent or "true" statements from the various teachings and practices described by prophets—either scriptural or contemporary: "as we know it in human terms, the 'full gospel' is not—and perhaps, given the apparently paradoxical nature of the universe itself, cannot ever be—a simple and clear set of unequivocal propositions."[20] Moreover, he asserts that Latter-day Saints should welcome the impossibility of reducing the gospel to simplistic perfection, because complexity and even apparent opposition have been the source of "the most important and productive ideas," "the energizing force in all art," and "the basis for success in all economic, political, and other social development."[21]

England proposes that "the Church is the best medium, apart from marriage (which it much resembles in this respect), for helping us gain salvation by grappling constructively with the oppositions of existence, despite our limited and various understandings of 'the gospel.'"[22] Citing Martin Luther's dictum that "marriage is the school of love," England describes the ways in which the church functions as a school where adherents can practice the Christian virtues they extol. Besides learning to appreciate and even love fellow congregants who are different from themselves, perhaps unlikely candidates for friendship, England suggests that the lay governing structure of the church gives members a chance to "be subject to leaders and occasionally to be hurt by their weakness and blindness" and learn to forgive, and then also have a chance to lead and discover how difficult it is, and learn to repent.[23]

England uses the example he frequently cited of David O. McKay, who was president of the church from 1951 until 1970, to illustrate the way that action can lead to belief, instead of the sequence we speak of more typically, with belief leading to religious activity.[24] England avers that he, too, experienced profound spiritual manifestations in the performance of his duties as a church member. He describes several examples from his time as the branch president of the congregation in Northfield, Minnesota, while he was working at St. Olaf College. In that capacity, England says, he saw the members of the branch "learn that the very exposures, exasperations, troubles, sacrifices, and disappointments that characterize involvement in a lay church like ours—and that are especially difficult for idealistic liberals to endure—are a main source of the Church's power to teach us to love."[25]

His emphasis on the church as a place to learn by practice the Christian virtues of charity, tolerance, patience, and humility leads England to a distinctive interpretation of the Apostle Paul's teachings about spiritual gifts. He describes several episodes when members of the congregation who were especially needy or difficult to work with helped those members of the congregation who had thought themselves more capable or more advanced in spiritual knowledge learn the lessons of sacrifice and self-abnegation that characterize Christian discipleship. "These are examples," England says, "of what Paul was talking about in 1 Corinthians 12, . . . where he teaches . . . that those with 'less honorable' and 'uncomely' gifts are *more* needed and more in need of attention and honor—perhaps because the *world* will automatically honor and use the others." He explains that the church is the proper school for learning these lessons, not in the abstract, but by practice; in church fellowship, those with the "more comely and world-honored gifts" can learn what they need to learn by patiently caring for and working alongside members who bring different gifts to the church community. Those who are used to feeling smart and capable will find themselves frustrated by the difficulties of applied Christian love.[26]

Finally, England links this insight back to the necessity of "opposition in all things." In this context, the important theme of the scripture for England is that the church is designed not always to ease the tensions and uncertainties of life, but sometimes actually to produce or intensify them:

> The Church is as "true" as—that is, as effective for salvation as—the gospel: the Church is where there is fruitful opposition, the place where its own revealed nature and inspired direction maintains an opposition between liberal and conservative values, faith and doubt, secure authority and frightening freedom, individual integrity and public responsibility—and thus where there will be misery as well as holiness, bad as well as good.
>
> . . . It is precisely in the struggle to be obedient while maintaining independence, to have faith while being true to reason and evidence, to serve and love in the face of imperfections, even offenses, that we can gain the humility we need to allow divine power to enter our lives in transforming ways. Perhaps the most amazing paradox about the Church is that it literally brings together the divine and the human . . . in concrete ways that no abstract systems of ideas ever could.[27]

England's refusal of the distinction between "gospel" and "church" is the ultimate expression of his belief that action is a vital path to knowledge, and that integrity consists not only in acting in accordance with one's beliefs, but also in forming beliefs through actions that test one's ethical reasoning and require risk and growth.

Despite the strong echo here of James's iteration of the risks of unbelief and the reward of risking belief, the only direct evidence of England's borrowing from James comes not from Witdsoe, but through B. H. Roberts, a brilliant autodidact who was a member of the Quorum of the Seventy (the governing body of the church ranking just below the Quorum of the Twelve). Roberts was an avid student of James's work, and incorporated it into the *Seventy's Course in Theology*, a study curriculum for men in the church. In his unpublished essay "The Lord's University?" (which will be discussed further in chapter 4), England cited Roberts's borrowing from James:

> We have some exciting statements by William James, the great American pragmatist, whom B. H. Roberts often quoted for his similarities to Mormon thinking and who was quite interested in Mormonism. Here is one example:
>
> Suppose that the world's author put the case to you before creation, saying: "I am going to make a world not certain to be saved, a world the perfection of which shall be conditional merely, the condition being that each several agent does its own "level best." I offer you the chance of taking part in such a world. Its safety, you see, is unwarranted. It is a real adventure, with real danger, yet it may win through. It is a social scheme of cooperative work genuinely to be done. Will you join the procession? Will you trust yourself and trust the other agents enough to face the risk?[28]

This prospect, said England, "warms the heart of every Mormon," because Mormons recognize this scenario as very close to Mormon teachings about a Council in Heaven, in which human beings, co-eternal with God, freely chose to participate in the project of building a moral world. England's assertion that James was "quite interested" in Mormonism may overstate the case, but James does mention Joseph Smith in *The Varieties of Religious Experience*, and he met with Mormon students and the president of Brigham Young Academy in 1892.[29] This conception of humanity's role in the divine project is key to England's theology and informs the disagreement over God's progression that drew England into conflict with Apostle Bruce McConkie, which will be discussed in detail in chapter 3.

It is not necessary to trace precisely the ways Roberts borrowed from James, only to note that Roberts, and later England, sensed resonance with Mormon teachings in James's affirmation of the individual's spiritual and moral standing, the possibility of discovering truth by an act of will, and the cosmic significance of human choices. To say that Eugene England is a Mormon liberal is, in part, to affirm England's perception that the theological and doctrinal resources of Mormonism could be compatible with a certain strain of American liberal thought, that the historical development of Mormon doctrine and practice in the direction of fundamentalism was not inevitable.

The Integrity of Mormon Literature

England regarded his scholarship, teaching, and personal writing as part of an integrated and dutiful life as a Latter-day Saint. He also quite directly linked his theological understanding with his approach to literature. Just as he championed a religious epistemology linked to ethical action, England's approach to literature prioritized the ethical and moral components of literary production and reception. In a review of the first anthology of Mormon literature, he wrote that Mormon creativity "shows to best advantage in various forms of personal witness to faith and experience, genres in which the truth of actual living, of quite direct confession, is at least as important as aesthetic or metaphorical truth—diaries, letters, sermons, lyric poetry (including hymns), autobiography and autobiographical fiction, and, increasingly, the personal essay."[30] In his first publication of his own personal essays, *Dialogues with Myself*, England set out "to show something of the range of subject matter and approach possible in the personal essay, to give a personal version of the intellectual and cultural history of Mormonism over the past twenty years, and, of course, to bear witness to the conditions of my own growth of mind and spirit during that period."[31]

Although he decries the merely didactic, England does seem convinced that artistic achievement and religious conviction are not always reconcilable. In a speech titled "Great Books or True Religion: Defining the New Mormon Scholar," England admits to a certain disinterest in the kinds of formal criticism in which an English professor of the era might have been expected to engage. He argues that "formalist criteria," like structure, style, organization, and so on, cannot account for the impact of some works on their audience. England prizes literature that "powerfully affected [him and his students] despite its obvious lack of formal or aesthetic perfection."[32]

England's focus on the effect of literature on the reader leads him to extol Mormon literature, broadly defined to include letters, journals, diaries, and so on, that reflects the vigor and health of the Mormon social experiment—Mormons' migration, settlement building, tithe-paying, irrigating, home teaching, churchgoing, welfare-system establishing—Mormons *doing something*. This literature, he claims, can affect its readers profoundly and have more impact in the world (even literature itself is required to *do something*!) than work that achieves excellence within traditional forms. Indeed, he warns that "at least in the twentieth century, the so-called 'great' literature has mainly been content to describe a morally barren or depraved contemporary landscape or has been based on a vision that has itself been shot through with moral or philosophical error."[33]

England loved and often quoted from the diary of Joseph Millett, an early Mormon convert, missionary, and settler. In "Great Books or True Religion," England cites several passages, noting Millett's "intuitive sense of significant detail and forthright revelation of self," his "simple but effective narrative skill and sense of drama," and "well-controlled humor and the sense of effective diction." One might quibble over whether the passages actually display these qualities, but it would be beside the point. England's argument about why Millett's diary is good literature is essentially an ethical argument, not an aesthetic one. For England, Millett's account may be called art because it is a vivid reflection of a good life, but the goodness is far more important than the artfulness. England qualifies his assertion that the ethical should replace the aesthetic as the most important criterion for judging literature, saying that he is "not suggesting didacticism as an adequate or even good criterion for literature; . . . not advocating a return to the pious moralizing that plagued Victorian literature" but nevertheless concludes, starkly, that an artist lacking "moral goodness" may create formally beautiful work that is particularly evil because of its aesthetic appeal. By contrast, the moral and ethical goodness of a work of art "will sometimes compensate for formal inadequacy or even give rise to more intuitive formal achievements; especially will this latter happen in unsophisticated and confessional forms like letters and journals, where the writer is able to project the fundamental and ultimately exemplary quality of life lived day by day."[34]

Sometimes, England's advocacy for the ethical evaluation of literature seems to dispense entirely with any aesthetic criteria. In a 1987 *BYU Studies* article about the journals of eight early apostles' missionary work in

England, he argues for reading the journals as both literature and potentially scripture. His title presages the argument: "A Modern Acts of the Apostles, 1840: Mormon Literature in the Making." He begins by proffering the Bible as an example of literature that both elites and ordinary readers can appreciate. He steers clear of typical categories of aesthetic judgment—the beautiful, the sublime—and focuses instead on "effective form and important content." It is not entirely clear what he means by "effective form," and he does not use the descriptor again in the article. It is a striking choice, however, in keeping with the existential restlessness England describes as compelling him to do or say something; literature, too, has to *do* something. Literature ought to consist of "significant experience, significantly expressed."[35] He offers a further gloss on "significant" expression—"expressed so as to affect our feelings, including our moral response to those important events, feelings, and ideas."

> What have I been reading? Significant experience, ideas, feelings, significantly expressed—that is, forcefully, memorably. We have the kind of insight literature gives to important historical events. . . . But we have in these Apostles' voices something else as well—accounts of their real involvement, their actual experiences with poverty, hate, and injustice, but also with divine direction, healings, and the effects on others of holding out to them their visions of temporal and spiritual salvation.[36]

The seamless conflation of literature and scripture is striking. Here, England is arguing for the literary quality of the journals as well as their religious significance, almost advocating both literary and scriptural canonization. Elsewhere, the process is reversed—he reads Shakespeare exactly as many people read scripture, as a source of moral and ethical guidance. Even a short list of a few of the titles of his essays on Shakespeare suggests the pattern: "Shakespeare and the At Onement of Jesus Christ," "The Quality of Mercy in Shakespeare," "Hamlet against Revenge." As their titles suggest, these essays are framed not by a literary critical apparatus, but by a straightforward thematic reading that seeks to derive ethical prescriptions.

England was an early advocate for attending to the narrative content of the Book of Mormon, and its effects on the reader, at a time when many LDS scholars of the Book of Mormon were still engaged in trying to find proofs for the ancient nature of the text and confirmation of Joseph Smith's account of its origins. In 1989, he published a devotional collection of writings submitted by members of the church from around the world about their encounters with the text.[37]

A few years before he died, England initiated another effort to document the ways that readers might encounter the Book of Mormon and encourage such engagement. The project, called *The Reader's Book of Mormon*, was completed and published after England's death by his friend and fellow *Dialogue* editor Robert Rees. The series was conceived in the image of the Pocket Canon edition of the Bible, with the scriptural texts introduced by a popular writer. England's instructions to the prominent LDS writers chosen to write the introductions was "to focus on the literary and religious qualities . . . rather than matters like historicity or technical theology and doctrine." He hoped the introductions would be "personal, compelling, even moving, thought-provoking but not argumentative ('critical' in the best sense)."[38] England chose to include the text of the Book of Mormon as it was first published in 1830, with the original chapter divisions and without breaks for verses. While England's approach was unusual when he proposed it, similar books have been widely accepted in the decade since its publication. Grant Hardy's *The Book of Mormon: A Reader's Edition*, which arranged the text in paragraphs and with special attention to poetic devices, was published by the University of Illinois Press in 2005, and BYU professor Royal Skousen published a critical edition of the original text with Yale University Press in 2009. Both were sold in Deseret Book, an LDS Church-owned bookstore whose stocklist carries an implied *nihil obstat* among devout Mormons. Beginning in 2020, BYU's Maxwell Institute is publishing a series of introductory works to accompany its own Study Edition of the Book of Mormon.

England's favorite English teacher at the University of Utah, Jack Adamson, taught classes on the Bible as literature in the 1970s. Adamson noted that there were two great sources of myth, which he defined as "a symbolic narrative which evokes awe and wonder and deals with the deepest concerns of [Western] culture"—the Greek and the Hebrew. He suggested that the Hebrew source (that is, the Bible) had become the more "potent" source in the mid-twentieth century.[39] Adamson was building on the work of literary critics whose work on myth and on the Bible became powerfully influential during the time that England was teaching literature—Erich Auerbach's *Mimesis* and Northrop Frye's *Anatomy of Criticism* both used biblical narratives as major texts for working out their critical theories.

England explicitly cites Frye, as well as French philosopher René Girard, in an essay on 1 Nephi, "Why Nephi Killed Laban: Reflections on the Truth of the Book of Mormon," though his application of their theories is surprising. England reads Frye's analysis of the Bible's typological literary structure as evidence of the book's divinity. Similarly, England reads in Girard's exegesis of biblical patterns of human and divine violence evidence of the Bible's revelatory character. He goes on to argue that, if the Book of Mormon contains similar typological structures and psychologically persuasive accounts of violence, then it, too, must be of divine origin: "the Book of Mormon attains similar qualities of form and content and thus stands as a second witness not only for Christ, but for the Logos, the redeemed and redeeming Word."[40]

England's appropriation of Frye, moreover, twists it to novel Mormon ends. England argues that among the functions of scripture is the revelation of divine patterns, for which humans yearn. England posits an underlying pattern that connects what is most deeply true in the universe with what humans perceive to be the unifying patterns of literature and scripture. He locates this fundamental pattern in what Frye calls the "Great Code": "It is the great scriptural pattern which, beyond what the universe is and has been, also images for us what life can be at its most satisfying, fulfilling, and enduring." Frye traces this code or metaphorical pattern through the Bible and Western literature, and England expansively argues that "Frye's most important claims for the Bible can also be demonstrated for the Book of Mormon."[41]

England takes the fact that the Book of Mormon can be read in the framework of Frye's "Great Code" as evidence of the book's divine origin and the truthfulness of its witness of Jesus. England analyzes the typological character of the Book of Mormon, pointing out that it deploys biblical imagery and patterns "with even greater intensity and consistency and ultimate significance than the Bible." Following Frye, England argues that these consistent patterns amplify the power of language to convey meaning beyond mere words. "That historical reality [what Frye calls, following Jacques Derrida, the history 'behind' the text] is, of course, the typological keystone, Christ's involvement with the world, and it is a reality that I think Frye senses, though he never quite admits, is uniquely saving."[42] Frye presumably doesn't "admit" the unique salvific power of Christ's involvement because he makes a distinction between reading literature and doing theology. But that is a distinction England does not make. He sees in scripture the same linguistic power that animates great literature. Scriptural texts, in England's reading, perform their most important function by "sustaining into the modern world the power of metaphorical language, to *all* our literature."

England's approach is somewhat similar to what French theorist and critic Pierre Bourdieu calls a "working-class" aesthetic: "working-class people expect every image to explicitly perform a function . . . and their judgments make reference, often explicitly, to the norms of morality or agreeableness. Whether rejecting or praising, their appreciation always has an ethical basis."[43]

One might also look to the German Romantics, particularly Friedrich Schiller, to ground this sort of ethical judgment of artistic merit, although England does not cite them (and, indeed, does not really make any attempt to ground his argument except in the framework of Mormon doctrine he presumes to share with his readers). The subject of England's dissertation, Frederick Tuckerman, as well as the American Transcendentalists whose work England knew well, would have been steeped in the German tradition. Schiller insisted that there was a moral component to the beautiful, and that the beauty of the human form was an expression of the "moralische Emfindungszustand"—the moral sensibility—of the human being's actions. A person in whom habitual right action had formed fine character might be beautiful regardless of her physical features. Where Immanuel Kant had posited the human *form* as the most truly beautiful object, because it is the most truly free, Schiller argues that the "architectonic beauty of the human form comes directly from nature and is formed by the rule of necessity."[44] The moral effect of the aesthetic object on the observing subject is also part of Schiller's criterion for beauty—the beautiful ought to evoke a moral sense of duty in the person who encounters it. German Romantics like Schiller were also interested in art's capacity for suspending various oppositions: between sensual enjoyment and spiritual exaltation, between expressive freedom and artistic form, for instance. "The beautiful" was defined, in part, as that which could create integrated objects and experience out of disparate human capacities.

Where England does resort to literary critical methods in his analysis, it is usually to reader-response theory. Briefly, reader-response theory is a method of reading texts that foregrounds the potential interaction with

the readers. Meaning is said to inhere not in the text itself, but in a negoti-
ated understanding created by the exchange between author and audience.
England applies this theory in the opening chapter of his 1992 book, *The
Quality of Mercy*. In that chapter, he argues that Shakespeare's *The Merchant
of Venice* is not, as most critics assert, an anti-Semitic text, drawing on ste-
reotypical portrayals of Jews, but a skillful deployment of the "bandwagon
effect," in which Shakespeare's audience is swept up in the tides of revenge
that carry the action of the play forward. When those revenge plots produce their inevitably tragic results, the audience is forced to reckon with
their own vengeful impulses. England describes the effect: "In each play a
moment comes when a morally sensitive audience, I believe, should start
to say, 'Hold on, this is going too far; let me off this bandwagon.' Then we
begin to ask ourselves whether the journey of revenge should ever have
begun, no matter how 'just,' and we start to consider the merits of mercy
instead."[45]

Similarly, his analysis of Nathaniel Hawthorne's short story "My Kinsman, Major Molineux," presented to a non-Mormon audience, analyzes the
thematic material of the story, draws historical and mythological parallels,
and then concludes with a discussion of the story's effect on its readers:

> Hawthorne's brilliance, and his worth to us, lies in his having captured the
> *experience* of that richer theology. . . . If we can respond to "My Kinsman"
> and thus be aided by a brilliant blending of all mankind's most power-
> ful mythic versions of the fortunate fall, we become again the original
> universal man and woman. . . . In our journey with Robin into ourselves,
> we also feel the new conviction that though our innocence has been lost,
> virtue and human solidarity are now *possible*. . . . We are strengthened
> to live maturely as flawed persons in a flawed world.[46]

We might recognize in this reading the methodology of Wolfgang Iser
or Roland Barthes, who built on poststructuralist theory by developing
literary critical tools focused on the ways in which readers participate in
the construction of a text's meaning. Given Latter-day Saints' fondness
for C. S. Lewis, and England's turning of the method toward ethical and
moral interpretation, it is perhaps more likely that England's exposure to
these methods came through Lewis's *Experiment in Criticism*. But Mormon
readers will also recognize the rhythms of the Sunday School classroom in
this approach—providing historical background, teasing out broad themes,

and then finding application to the lives of class members is the method of scripture study almost reflexively deployed by Mormons. It is based in part on a passage in the Book of Mormon, where the prophet Nephi explains that he expects his audience (in that case, his brothers) to read themselves into the canonical accounts of the Pentateuch and the prophecies of Isaiah: "And I did read many things unto them which were written in the books of Moses; but that I might more fully persuade them to believe in the Lord their Redeemer I did read unto them that which was written by the prophet Isaiah; for I did liken all scriptures unto us, that it might be for our profit and learning."[47]

Many academics would bristle at having their hermeneutic compared to Sunday School exegesis, but perhaps England would not mind. He was always skeptical of literary theory—from one of his earliest speeches at BYU, when he said that he had "come to be increasingly uneasy with the perspectives of formalist literary criticism in which I was trained under some of the great masters of such criticism," to one of his last talks at BYU, where he evinced distrust of both "the newer criticisms' liberal inclination to social and political activism" and "the older criticisms' conservative inclination to ignore the ethical and political implications of literature."[48] He often spoke of the freedom he felt at BYU to collapse academic and religious categories, as in this address to the Phi Beta Kappa chapter at BYU: "You have a much greater amount here of what is the most important academic freedom, in my opinion, the freedom to express and discuss openly your *positive* religious and moral views and convictions rather than merely your negative ones or your criticism."[49] One of his colleagues, in describing him as a teacher, emphasized that "it is the particular gift of Eugene England through his confrontations with experience and literature, both scriptural and secular, to provoke us to examine our own beliefs, experiences, and their meanings in our lives—to find our own questions and endure our own answers."[50]

In articulating these criteria for evaluating literature, England was also part of a maturing tradition of Mormon literature. The first anthology of Mormon literature was published in 1979, by Richard Cracroft and Neal Lambert, both professors in the English Department at BYU. They noted, as England did, that the struggles of the early Latter-day Saints had evoked writing that was "often less concerned with the aesthetics of form and style than it is with the practical matters of defense, instruction, preachment, and encouragement."[51] Cracroft and Lambert posit that the Mormon literary tradition is "outside the mainstream of modern literary fashion" mostly because it is optimistic, reflective of a practical theology that leaves little room for the kind of existential uncertainty that drove many twentieth-century literary projects. "Mormons characteristically continue to see the world through a paradisiacal glass, brightly. . . . This God-centered world view is seen as the source of great human responsibility, dignity, and opportunity, a desirable kind of world view that seems to be finding more and more adherents in a world fraught with a debilitating purposelessness."[52]

In his review of this volume, England criticized it only for being "too apologetic" about the quality of Mormon literature. He echoed and even amplified Cracroft and Lambert's claims about the spiritual healthiness that characterizes Mormon literature, and elaborated on the criteria by which Mormon literature ought to be evaluated:

> Our assessment must include the literal truth of the religious and moral vision expressed and the rightness of the religious and moral response evoked. . . . Our literature must not be subjected to the traps laid by various forms of cultural relativism—especially those rampant in psychological and mythological criticism and in regionalism: I mean the tendency to create as writers, and then describe as critics, structures of thought and experience and perspectives of life which are implicitly valued mainly because complex or paradoxical or exotic—or for mere correspondence to archetypal (or Freudian, etc.) categories, without reference to any kind of ultimate or historical truth.[53]

England's practical, applied, and frankly moralistic approach to literary texts is not merely evidence of his theoretical and methodological independence from his training or from trends in academic literary criticism. It would not have been a fashionable approach in English departments of the 1970s, but England's ideas could have been articulated in terms that would have been recognized and appreciated by his academic peers, by more explicitly relying on reader-response theories or articulating some neo-Romantic framework. Instead, England's approach is grounded in the unitary Mormon consciousness that he learned in his father's wheatfield. His work was not farming, but reading English literature, and he meant to consecrate that labor just as his father had consecrated his harvest.

Integrity and Form: The Personal Essay

In their foreword to *A Believing People*, Cracroft and Lambert forecast that "as the Church finds itself increasingly at odds with the moral values of the encroaching world, the personal essay will undoubtedly assume a larger role as a vehicle for the expression of the values of a people as manifest in the individual life of a sensitive writer."[54] In his review of the volume, England cited this passage approvingly: "I hope the editors are right, because for our time and for the widest possible appreciation by readers and participation by writers I believe the personal essay is the form that best suits the particular needs and possibilities of a literature for 'a believing people.'"[55]

The personal essay appealed to England as a literary mode that allowed the expression of an integrated Mormon life—theologically informed reflection, moral action, faithful introspection, and aesthetic striving. The essay as form allows, almost requires, the integrated, usually first-person voice of the narrator. It allows the author's effort to be visible to the reader, and openly, actively invites the reader's participation. It allows doubt and indecision and imperfection in its creative progression. It is not difficult to draw the parallels to the most optimistic strains of Mormon theology in a literary form that lays bare the stuff of human agency and choice. England finds warrant for privileging the essay in the Mormon "theological emphasis on life as a stage where the individual self is both tested and created, and our history of close self-examination in journals and testimony-bearing."[56] For England, the essay is the form that can most fully represent the varied activities of the mind—vigorous thinking, but also believing and hoping and striving.

England not only highlighted the potential of personal essays to reflect and illuminate Mormon life, he actively championed the writing and publishing of essays. From the beginning, the journal England helped to create, *Dialogue*, devoted a sizable portion of its pages to the personal essay. England also encouraged the publication of essays in *Exponent II*—a newspaper founded by Mormon feminists in 1974—and *Sunstone*, a magazine that also published its first issue in 1974, as a forum for Mormon experience, scholarship, issues, and art.

By 1982, both personal and critical essays were flourishing in Mormon publications, and England coedited a volume called *Tending the Garden: Essays on Mormon Literature*. In her chapter focused on the personal essay,

Mary Bradford (who was one of England's successors as editor of *Dialogue*) was able to cite dozens of her favorite essays to highlight the features of the form as it was evolving in the hands of Mormon writers.[57]

Besides creating venues for publishing essays, England encouraged students and friends to *write* essays and submit them for publication. His student Gideon Burton, now himself a professor of English at BYU, recalled,

> After I mused about the ideal kinds of writing and writers I thought our LDS community needed, Gene commented—both casually and sincerely—that maybe I could fill that need. As he did for so many, Gene made me feel that I had something to say, and his own writings gave me a model for how to say it. . . . Anyone with ties to Mormonism who wrote in a personal or literary way would find himself or herself gently woven into Gene's narrative of an evolving and improving LDS literary tradition.[58]

England's championing of the personal essay appears to have been prescient. He could not have predicted the explosion of personal writing that the internet would enable. But he was right to identify the testimony-bearing impulse that is instilled in Mormons from the time they are assigned to give their first "talk" in Primary (the Sunday meeting for children) at age three as the germ of self-conscious storytelling from personal experience that grows into the autobiographical forms of literary reflection that he identified as the locus of Mormons' best potential contributions. The proliferation, beginning a few years after his death, of Mormon blogs, with their thousands upon thousands of little essays, would probably have both delighted and worried him. Delighted, because the spirited (in every sense of the word) discussion of Mormon topics was exactly the kind of dialogue he craved; worried, because despite his ceaseless encouragement of liberality of expression, he was also somewhat conservative with regard to form. The lack of editing and free-for-all nature of online publishing would have brought England's enthusiasm for plunging in and doing something into conflict with his dedication to careful writing and rewriting. His own essays went through many drafts and were frequently revised, sometimes over decades.

Late in his career, England was influenced by his appreciation of feminist literary criticism. He praised Mormon women for the quality of their literary voices—"honest, meek, and thus more genuinely powerful, prophetic voice"—asserting that Mormon women have always written this way and thus produced more good writing.[59] Despite the slightly embarrassing essentialism, this notion that the personal essay was best seen as a "feminine" form led to some interesting formal experimentation in England's later essays. "Easter Weekend," "Jacaranda," "Monte Cristo," and a few others are especially free, sliding between autobiography, travelogue, epistle, prayer, flashback, and lyrical description with fluidity that requires both concentration and a willing suspension of temporality and logic from the reader.

> My best piece of writing so far, I believe (and more objective critics have agreed), is a personal essay called "Easter Weekend" (1988). In writing it, I began to discover the "woman" in myself, a voice that hovered and circled rather than thrusting to conclusions, that combined narratives like a mosaic to get at emotional patterns rather than moving through logical exposition to a rational conclusion. With increasing assurance, I listened for and finally heard and expressed new voices, different from my own but part of me. No, I don't believe women naturally write that way or that all men should. I only know that I discovered important things, things I am excitedly exploring, that cultural male modes and models had not provided me.[60]

There are a thousand reasons, of course, to wish that England had lived longer, but unsatisfied curiosity about the forms England's writings might have essayed, given time and ripeness, is surely one of the many reasons to mourn his untimely passing.

CHAPTER 3

The Possibilities of Dialogue

Dialogue will not solve all of our intellectual and spiritual
problems—and it will not save us; but it can bring us joy and
new vision and help us toward that dialogue with our deepest
selves and with our God which can save us.

—Eugene England, "The Possibility of Dialogue: A Personal
View," *Dialogue: A Journal of Mormon Thought*

This passage from the first issue of *Dialogue: A Journal of Mormon Thought*,
founded by England and other students and professors at Stanford in 1966,
is one iteration of a central focus of England's thought, and it reflects a core
aspect of his personality and a source of his profound influence on generations of Latter-day Saints. Every remembrance of England mentions his love
of conversation and his passionate need for interlocutors. England's treatment of Shakespeare, of the authors of the Book of Mormon, and of Joseph
Smith and other Mormon thinkers almost always puts them in dialogue
with each other, or with their imagined readers. His poems are frequently
explicitly addressed to someone, often voiced in the second person. He
seems to have often wanted to work through his thoughts in dialogue—his
correspondence often includes requests for comments on his work, and he
saved many drafts of his essays with friends' and colleagues' marginal notes
as well as his own. Dialogue was not just a trendy buzzword for England;
it was a central organizing principle of his life and work.

In many contexts, the notion that dialogue is a productive way of arriv-
ing at shared understanding is not particularly radical. But in the Mormon
context of the second half of the twentieth century, it was not an anodyne
concept. The possibility of knowledge as dialectic is deeply rooted in the
strain of Mormon thought that asserts both the salvific potential of human
community and the individual's right to unmediated communication with
God. At the same time, it is in tension with other foundational Mormon as-
sertions about the authority of prophets and the requirement that individual

revelation, conscience, and logic be subordinated to priestly authority. This chapter will examine the possibilities and limitations of a dialogical approach to Mormonism by elaborating England's conception of dialogue and detailing the ways in which he instantiated his commitment to dialogue in conversation, letters, and publishing forums he helped to create.

Defining Dialogue

England found scriptural warrant for his ideas about dialogue in the Apostle Paul's injunction to the Thessalonians: "Prove all things; hold fast that which is good." In the phrase "prove all things," England read the productive skepticism of the Enlightenment—the kind of curiosity and willingness to overturn dogma that had led to scientific discovery and new conceptions of human possibility, including various civil rights movements. In the phrase "hold fast that which is good," England found a bulwark against skepticism turned to corrosive cynicism. Dialogue, he argued, required people to be willing to commit to the good and true things they discovered in their searching and doubt.

Importantly, England is not speaking of a dialectic on either the Platonic model, in which the teacher challenges the student's hypotheses, leading her gradually to a view similar to the teacher's, or the Hegelian model, in which any given position calls for confrontation with a position with which it is in tension, leading to ever more comprehensive understanding. England uses "dialogue" in the simplest sense of an exchange of ideas between people—a conversation. His notion of dialogue also does not require a resolution or synthesis. Closely related to both his ideas about paradox and about the essay, "dialogue" allows contradictions to stand and tensions to remain unresolved. It is an open-ended exploration of ideas that may amplify or cancel each other at various points. In speaking of a colleague with whom he had painfully disagreed, and then been reconciled enough to have more productive disagreements, England wrote, "I say, God give us all the courage to be as honest and pure as this dear colleague and thus to make the church a place of healing and peace-making, not by ignoring differences or errors, but by loving and talking despite them."[1]

England's commitment to dialogue seems to have come first from a temperamental disposition to learn by working through ideas with others, a simple pleasure in the kinds of serious conversations his boyhood friends recall, and in the study and discussion groups he was already organizing in high school. Later, dialogue was a necessary way of getting along with those in the church with whom he sometimes disagreed over religious questions, and often disagreed with over political views. In his congregation in Palo Alto, for instance, he recalled a time when he gave a talk about causes he felt the Christian gospel compelled him to champion.[2] The next week, another member of the ward stood at the pulpit to refute England's sermon point by point. England was furious and hurt, but decided to go to the man's house and try to be reconciled. England described the meeting as "awkward and painful at first," but it ended with the two men becoming friends, and learning from their disagreements: "Though he disagreed with me about many things, he was willing to improve the dialogue and learning in my [Sunday School] class through gracious opposition, because he knew my basically conservative faithfulness."[3]

Later still, England began to articulate what he called a "theology of diversity," which required dialogic interaction with an esteemed other as a means of growth toward godliness. He relied strongly on the Book of Mormon theology developed in 2 Nephi, which declares that "there must needs be an opposition in all things," and even (on England's reading) makes this oppositional ontology a condition of God's existence:

> If not so . . . righteousness could not be brought to pass, neither wickedness, neither holiness nor misery, neither good nor bad. Wherefore, all things must needs be a compound in one; wherefore, if it should be one body it must needs remain as dead, having no life neither death, nor corruption nor incorruption, happiness nor misery, neither sense nor insensibility.
>
> Wherefore, it must needs have been created for a thing of naught; wherefore there would have been no purpose in the end of its creation. Wherefore, this thing must needs destroy the wisdom of God and his eternal purposes, and also the power, and the mercy, and the justice of God.
>
> . . . And if these things are not there is no God. And if there is no God we are not, neither the earth; for there could have been no creation of things, neither to act nor to be acted upon; wherefore, all things must have vanished away.[4]

England's gloss of this passage in *Why the Church Is as True as the Gospel* calls it

> perhaps the most provocative and profound statement of abstract theology in the scriptures, because it describes what apparently is most

ultimate in the universe. In context it clearly suggests that not only is contradiction and opposition a natural part of human experience, something God uses for his redemptive purposes, but that opposition is at the very heart of things: it is *intrinsic* to the two most fundamental realities, intelligence and matter. . . . According to Lehi, opposition provides the universe with energy and meaning, even makes possible the existence of God and everything else.[5]

This scripture is foundational to England's epistemology, ecclesiology, and even his theology. In an essay published in 1994, titled "No Respecter of Persons: A Mormon Ethics of Diversity," England offered the union between man and woman as the paradigmatic example of this kind of complementarity, and described the Mormon doctrine of a Heavenly Mother as "a keystone concept in the crucial theology of diversity . . . because it establishes genuine diversity as intrinsic to the very nature of Godhead."[6] The stakes of dialogue could not be higher. For England the intimate other is necessary not only for working through quotidian ethical questions and practical learning, but for the kind of salvific growth that is the purpose of human life.

The Possibility of Mormon Dialogue

While England's thought is thoroughly grounded in Mormon scripture, it also runs up against unresolved tensions in Mormon history and practice— questions about how a church founded on the possibility of an open canon, ongoing revelation, and individual access to the divine can function as a coherent institution. In its origins, Mormonism shared the anti-creedalism of New England's primitive gospel movement, a loose conglomeration of religious seekers who shared a few core beliefs, including the notion that religion should be personal and individual, independent of clergy and formally organized churches. Primitive gospel proponents rejected the kinds of formal dogma that distinguished various Christian denominations, preferring to organize around charismatic individuals who had dialogic relationships with God. Joseph Smith's parents and grandparents, as well as many early adherents of the movement organized around Joseph Smith's revelations, shared this anti-creedal stance, believing strongly in Joseph's ability to receive truth through an ongoing conversation with the divine. For the first decade or so of the church's existence, it produced few written doctrinal statements.

However, as the church grew—and, indeed, as part of the mechanism of that growth—pamphleteering became a prominent mode of communicating the new church's message. As a result, the anti-dogmatic impulses of the earliest Latter-day Saints gave way to an increasingly formalized collection of beliefs, which were found in pamphlets, newspapers, and canonized transcriptions of Joseph Smith's sermons and revelatory documents like the Lectures on Faith—a set of lectures delivered in the "School of the Elders" in the winter of 1834–35 in an early attempt to systematize Latter-day Saint theology.[7] However, Joseph Smith did not himself write many of these statements—some were dictated through scribes, but missionaries, especially in England, had significant autonomy and often published their own doctrinal interpretations in various quasi-official outlets. The Lectures on Faith were probably authored largely by Sidney Rigdon. Even hymnals and texts that would later be canonized appeared in multiple, often dissimilar editions. The proliferation of printed doctrine only rarely led to conflict with church leadership.

Still, Joseph Smith attempted to formalize governance of the church and dissemination of doctrine in a mode that did not rely entirely on personal charisma. In the very first issue of *Dialogue: A Journal of Mormon Thought*, Catholic scholar Mario De Pillis described Joseph's attempts to establish "a sect to end all sects." Smith's quest for religious *authority*, De Pillis argues, was always in tension with the also persistent Mormon teaching that every believer could communicate directly with the Deity, as Joseph Smith had. De Pillis describes the Mormon God as friendlier and more scrutable God than that of the Calvinists, but just as absolute in some ways, particularly in the requirement of ecclesiastical authority. There is no "priesthood of all believers" in Joseph Smith's thinking, despite his own experience of personal theophany in response to a question about which church he should join. According to De Pillis, "Joseph Smith hoped to establish the authority of what the early Mormons called 'the one true church' over against the theological potpourri of competing sects that surrounded him as a young man in the Burned-over District. Later elaborations of doctrine never obscured this goal. New revelations merely reinforced the uniqueness of the one true church."[8] Ecclesiastical authority also came to mean the authority to interpret scripture and revelation for the church, but the mechanisms by which that control is exercised were slow to develop and still operate unevenly. As long as the church was geographically contained and isolated, tight-knit communities and personal relationships usually sufficed to rein in doctrinal disputes (with notable exceptions, some of which are discussed below). The church was still anti-creedal enough that doctrinal purity was less of a concern than personal loyalty—the looseness of Mormon theology allowed for a great deal of minor heresy among those who called themselves Saints. In the early twentieth century, Mormons seemed willing, even eager, to assimilate new ideas from religious, scientific, and economic developments in American culture.

Around the turn of the twentieth century, young Latter-day Saints began leaving Utah in significant numbers to study in Eastern universities: James E. Talmage, who became the president of the University of Utah and wrote influential books on Mormon theology (including *Jesus the Christ* and *The Articles of Faith*), studied geology at Lehigh University and Johns Hopkins University. John A. Widtsoe, who became president of Utah State University and then an apostle, studied chemistry at Harvard and the University of Göttingen. His book *Joseph Smith as Scientist* was the recommended curriculum for the young men's and young women's organizations of the church in 1909.[9] William H. Chamberlain attended summer sessions at the University of Chicago Divinity School in 1902 and 1903, and became a teacher of ancient languages and philosophy at Brigham Young University. Sidney Sperry, a teacher of high school scripture study courses ("Seminary" in LDS parlance) went to the University of Chicago Divinity School *against* the advice of church leaders in 1925. Upon his return, he was such an effective teacher that official attitudes toward divinity school education began to change. In 1930, Daryl Chase, Russel Swensen, and George Tanner were given a "calling" by church leaders to attend the Divinity School at the University of Chicago. Swensen recalled that William Harper, the president of the school,

> laid down some interesting guidelines for the University and the Divinity School that still persist. His major emphasis was complete academic freedom, rigorous and productive research, and the avoidance of religious controversy. It was a time when the fundamentalist-modernist controversy was raging, but in my four years at the Divinity School I do not remember hearing any church or rival scholars harshly or unfairly criticized. Because of this emphasis on research the Divinity School was noted more for its scholarly publications than for its devotional or promotional religious activities.[10]

An additional seven LDS students attended the University of Chicago Divinity School during the 1930s, all of them returning to Utah and teaching at universities or in the Church Educational System. After the 1930s, the flow of students to Chicago abruptly stopped. Swensen speculated that change might have been due to general authorities' suspicion "that the sociological, historical, and literary approach to Bible studies plus the liberal spirit of the Divinity School would undermine the faith and loyalty of L.D.S. students who went there to study."[11]

Swensen's surmise that church leaders may have feared that divinity school would weaken the faith of LDS students is notable, particularly since the effect on the students at the University of Chicago had been demonstrably the opposite. Despite the fact that the curriculum at the Divinity School had studiously avoided the modernist controversy, however, this debate had made its way into Mormon consciousness. There had been significant conflict at Brigham Young University and the University of Utah, mostly over the teaching of the theory of evolution in science classes.[12] Generally, conflicts over evolution could be fought to an uneasy truce in which religious authorities declared that God had intentionally created human beings in his image as his children, even if the mechanisms of Creation were mysterious, which allowed scientists enough room to cautiously embrace scientific discoveries. Still, conflict between religious and scholarly authority continued. In 1934, James Talmage's son, Sterling, questioned Apostle Joseph Fielding Smith's pseudoscientific exegesis of Joshua 10:15, in which the sun stood still. Talmage, a geology professor at BYU, was convinced that Smith's attempts to explain the miraculous event in terms that sounded scientific would be damaging to young people who needed to know that "our faith is not founded on absurdity." Talmage argued that religion and science ought to occupy separate spheres, and that Smith should confine his public opinions to the religious realm in which he had authority, and leave science to those with the scientific experience and authority to make pronouncements in that sphere. Smith replied,

> I have not felt that I am under any obligation to accept the theories which are based on scientific research, but have the divine right to question them. I am, however, under obligation to accept revealed truth which comes through the opening of the heavens from the One who "comprehendeth all things," and when I find what I believe to be a conflict between the theories of men and the word of the Lord, I am bold to say

that I accept the latter with full confidence that the theories must be changed.[13]

Fear of the faith-diluting effects of encounters with modernist theory might have been related to other events, as well. During the same period, a group of Mormon writers whom Edward Geary later called "Mormondom's Lost Generation" left Utah for training in literature and did not return to their Mormon faith, instead writing about their Mormon roots in both nostalgic and critical works like *Children of God: An American Epic* (Vardis Fisher), *A Little Lower Than the Angels* (Virginia Sorensen), and *The Giant Joshua* (Maureen Whipple).[14]

As Latter-day Saints became more fully integrated into American society, church leaders increasingly felt the need to establish and maintain doctrinal coherence. Teachings of church leaders in the Utah period that seemed speculative or radical were abandoned, though not usually formally. Rather, emphasis in official materials quietly shifted as the church sought to establish itself as a modernizing American denomination. Under the administration of Joseph F. Smith (1901–1918), church authorities began working to regularize church practices. Everything from ritual healing practices to weeknight activity programs for teenagers was reviewed in an effort to encourage uniformity. Beginning in 1907, a committee called the Committee of Correlation and Adjustments was formed to evaluate and coordinate the activities of church units and auxiliaries (including, for instance, the women's auxiliary called the Relief Society; the Sunday School organization; the children's auxiliary, Primary; and the auxiliaries for teenage boys and girls, which changed names several times during those decades). The committee aimed to "prevent duplication of roles and lesson material, develop teacher training, and establish a unified church magazine." By 1913, the committee started work on curriculum materials, suggesting that "the Primary Association and MIA [youth auxiliary] would deal with practical religion, secular subjects, and recreation, and Religion Classes, Sunday School, and the Aaronic Priesthood [an organization for young men] would teach scriptural topics and church history."[15]

These efforts at control and rational organization proceeded with varying success through the next several decades, interrupted to some degree by other priorities during the Great Depression and World Wars. The growth of the church—its membership more than doubled in the first half of the twentieth century—required continued efforts to maintain centralized control, especially over teaching materials and church-published resources for missionaries and congregations outside of the intermountain West. In the early 1960s, as the church's growth accelerated, the Correlation Committee undertook its most concerted and programmatic effort to streamline church teachings and publications. Sunday School manuals and curricular materials for women's, children's, and youth auxiliaries were brought under the control of the committee.[16] Formerly independent publications like the *Relief Society Magazine*, which had been published by and for LDS women, and contained both official curricular materials and more general items of interest to women, were consolidated under the aegis of the committee, as were all of the independently published international magazines for church members.[17]

Thus it was in a particularly unfavorable context for independent publishing that England decided to undertake the creation of a new independent journal. By 1965, England and others had been talking for years about the possibility of a publication aimed at thoughtful Mormons who might want greater intellectual exploration of LDS teachings than were typically found in Sunday School. Wesley Johnson, who became one of the first editors of *Dialogue*, recalls mentioning the possibility in a Sacrament Meeting sermon in 1959, and receiving an enthusiastic response. Mary Bradford remembered England discussing a similar idea as an undergraduate at the University of Utah.[18] Johnson and England both ended up at Stanford University in the early 1960s, Johnson as a history professor and England as a graduate student in the English Department. They did not know each other until a mutual friend, Diane Monson, to whom each had mentioned his idea about a new publication, introduced them. After their first meeting, and with support from other friends—notably Frances Menlove, Paul Salisbury, and Joseph Jeppson—England and Johnson began planning in earnest.[19]

The name *Dialogue* was England's idea.[20] It was readily adopted by the group of founders, and captured their hope that it would be a forum for discussion from many points of view. From the beginning, they hoped to counter the impression held by those, like Dallin H. Oaks—a University of Chicago law professor who would become president of BYU (in 1971) and then an apostle (in 1984)—who had heard that this was "a rather leftish outfit."[21] They sought out orthodox voices, and tried to enlist BYU professors and Church Educational System faculty to serve on the board. The results of their efforts were mixed—Oaks served on the board for three years,[22] while Kenneth Godfrey, a CES employee, initially agreed, but resigned at the urging of his boss before the publication of the first issue. With the Correlation movement in full swing, and strong emphasis from the official church on establishing proper channels for review and ecclesiastical approval of publications about church teachings, many were skeptical of an independent publication, regardless of its content. Hugh Nibley, a scholar of ancient languages and widely respected BYU professor, wrote a letter to Apostle Ezra Taft Benson discouraging the idea of the journal. His concerns seem to have been related more to the proposed title and dialectical format than with the mere idea of an independent publication. A few years earlier, Nibley had written to BYU philosophy professor Chauncy Riddle that "all churches but ours publish serious journals frankly dealing with things from their own point of view. . . . It is the right and duty of those who have a word to say above the adolescent level about the Gospel to publish their findings."[23] Now, although he credited the faithfulness of the editors and board of *Dialogue*, and acknowledged that "there are some issues that can be most profitably treated by hearing from both sides," he nevertheless concluded that "the title of the journal displays both its strength and its fatal weakness. Christ often rebuked his Apostles both before and after the Resurrection, for making a Dialogue of the Gospel. The word appears 31 times in the New Testament and always in a bad sense."[24]

Dialogue board members sought to allay these concerns by letting members of the Quorum of the Twelve and the First Presidency know about their plans. England favored personal meetings with all of them, but was persuaded by Richard Bushman's argument that face-to-face visits would be more likely than letters to elicit explicit disapproval. Bushman favored sending a letter only to the First Presidency, arguing that the more apostles they informed, the more likely they would be to receive at least one unfavorable response. In the end, they sent letters to each member of the Quorum of the Twelve and the First Presidency, explaining that *Dialogue* would "display the rich intellectual and spiritual resources of the Gospel as mature men have discovered them and how relevant our faith is to contemporary life. The content of the magazine will be proof that a Latter-day Saint need not abandon thought to be a faithful Church member nor his faith to be thoughtful."[25]

England expected that church leaders' reactions would be positive: "I just assumed they would approve. I saw our project as wholly in accord with the church's mission, and a contribution to it." Most of the direct responses of General Authorities were neutral, or mildly critical, like a letter from S. Dilworth Young, a Seventy (the governing body just below the Quorum of the Twelve Apostles in authority), who did not criticize anything particular in the first issue, but cautioned that "liberals" might try to pressure the journal to include content that was not "the solid opinion of the leaders of the church, past or present." "If you do resist [them]," Young cautioned, "they likely will brand you as prejudiced, and with that brand on you, you will likely try to remove the brand by proving you are not. . . . Remember that undeviating loyalty to the church leaders (1st Pres[idenc]y and the Twelve) is the only standard you can maintain if you want the approbation of the church."[26]

More negative reactions came indirectly from people who had promised contributions, including Elder Marion D. Hanks (a member of the Seventy) and BYU professor Robert Thomas, who hinted that he had heard from General Authorities that they did not approve of participation in *Dialogue*'s endeavor. This kind of indirect disapproval has continued throughout *Dialogue*'s existence, punctuated only occasionally by official criticism. As the church grew, the emphasis on the appearance of unanimity among top leaders meant that they took part less often in the kinds of open or public doctrinal disputes that nineteenth- and early twentieth-century leaders had engaged in, and doctrinal conflict was largely outsourced to leaders at the ward and stake level, or to a growing class of professional church administrators.

In retrospect, and in the context of the authority structure of the church as it developed in the late twentieth century, England's expectation that church authorities would appreciate his efforts may seem either foolishly optimistic or shockingly naïve. At the time, and given England's experiences with church leaders throughout his life, it was neither. The unexpectedly negative response of church leaders to the founding of *Dialogue* points up the critical moment in which England lived and worked; he found himself on the fault line between Mormonism as a regional communitarian church and Mormonism as a worldwide church with strong centralized authority over both doctrine and procedure.

England was among the last Mormons to retain an emotional sense of the old, tight-knit intermountain church that made him feel confident addressing General Authorities. His father was acquainted and friendly with many of the Apostles, at a time when they still occasionally went golfing with their neighbors. Eugene England Jr. and Charlotte England were part of the wave of outmigration and growth that changed the LDS Church from a relatively small, isolated sect at the beginning of the twentieth century to a rapidly growing worldwide church at the century's end. In the introduction to a large oral history project tracing this migration, Wesley Johnson and Marian Ashby Johnson compare the situation of Latter-day Saints at the beginning and end of the twentieth century:

> In 1900, Mormons were predominantly rural, not very well educated, not very wealthy, relatively provincial in outlook, with very little national influence, standing apart from American society. By the year 2000, Mormons had become mainly urban, living in large metropolitan areas, often highly educated, many quite prosperous, assimilated into the American mainstream, spread across the continent with less than a third of them residing in the traditional Mormon Corridor [the area of nineteenth-century Mormon settlement, extending from Colonia Juarez in northern Mexico, through Utah, western Wyoming, and eastern Idaho, north to Cardston, Alberta, Canada].[27]

As young Mormons left Utah for military service or schooling, they were exposed to a broader range of their fellow Americans, and discovered that they had more in common with their "Gentile" neighbors than they might have expected.[28] The Johnsons quote Ned Hill, who left Utah for graduate school and became a faculty member at Cornell and Indiana universities. He said that "it was wonderful to know that there were awfully good people who were Catholics, Jews, or atheists—people of very different backgrounds. We developed dear, dear friends whom we still interact with today." This was a common finding in the Johnsons' research, "repeated hundreds of times in the project's interviews."[29] Ties to the theocratic and communitarian Mormonism, which had been gradually attenuated through the early part of the twentieth century, were stretched to breaking by the assimilation of this new generation of Mormon "expatriates." Even those who, like the Englands, returned to their Mormon homelands, brought a new perspective on the safe valleys in which they had been raised.

Another important experience for young Mormons who left settled Mormon communities was that they became leaders of fledgling Mormon congregations in their new homes. England's experience of being called as a branch president before he was forty years old, which would have been somewhat unusual in Utah or Idaho, was repeated throughout the country where Mormon outmigrants and missionaries gathered new congregations.

The nature of church leadership also changed as congregations multiplied. These bishops and other local leaders had less personal contact with General Authorities than those of the previous generation, but depended on them more, as direction for managing church programs came increasingly from Salt Lake City. In the second half of the twentieth century, it was not only the geographic distance between General Authorities and bishops, branch presidents, and stake presidents that increased; the central leadership of the church had to become a governing bureaucracy for a worldwide church, rather than advisors to the shepherds of familiar flocks. England's efforts at dialogue with church leaders reflect both the familiarity that characterized those relationships in the early decades of the century, and the organizational distance that reshaped them throughout the twentieth century.

Dialogue in Letters

Beginning in his graduate school years, perhaps because of his father's friendly association with church leaders, England exchanged letters with several current and future members of the Quorum of the Twelve and other General Authorities. These epistolary dialogues with LDS authorities highlight not only the varying degrees to which theological dialogue can be productive, but also the ways in which England pushes intuitively against the deepest tensions in Mormon theology and ecclesiology. England's correspondence with General Authorities was extensive, but the letters with Elder Marion D. Hanks, Neal A. Maxwell, and Bruce R. McConkie are particularly instructive.

England's letters with Hanks are immediately very personal, even intimate. England had been one of Hanks's students when Hanks was an instructor in the University of Utah Institute of Religion, prior to his call as a Seventy. In a letter written during England's graduate studies, Hanks offered avuncular admonishment:

> You know how to be happy and how not to be happy. Make up your mind and be happy. You know me well enough to know that I am not suggesting that you close your eyes or your mind, or that the road out isn't always going to be there. I am just suggesting that your highest happiness will be found lifting and deepening and broadening and loving, and not standing on the edge making strange noises or asking questions that any fool can ask while others with maybe fewer answers are inside doing the work.[30]

England was taken aback at the characterization of him that this advice seemed to imply, and wrote frankly in response:

> I must admit that your letter disturbed me, especially whe[re] it seemed to carry the tone of one on the inside speaking to one on the "edge," or to the Gene that is still a wild-eyed adolescent idealist or a naively crusading Samoan missionary. I'm not those things. . . . I love the Lord and his Kingdom with all my heart. Every day I bet my eternal life on the principles of His Gospel and the practices of His Church. I think and act within a specific context of Mormon faith that defines my life and creates my soul. I relate to my wife and raise my children and use my time in terms of the counsel of the Prophet and the heritage of Mormon experience. . . . And if you really think, as your letter seems to imply, that if I have questions and recognize abysses when they appear then I am not happy and not engaged with all my soul in "lifting and deepening and broadening and loving"—especially when they are questions and abysses that the moral exactness of Christ himself and his prophets and your own teachings and example encourage me to face—if you really think that, then I just plain don't understand.[31]

Later, their correspondence included real anger and misunderstanding over an episode in England's Institute class at Stanford, in which the discussion disturbed some members so much that they contacted Elder Hanks about it. Hanks let England know about these complaints, and England seems to have responded by discussing the episode with his class and asking them to come to him directly with any complaints in the future. Classmates took sides and Elder Hanks also heard about the ensuing unpleasantness from one of the class members. His next letter to England was a harsh admonishment, expressing "disgust" and very personal anger. England's reply was defensive, but also anguished. A few weeks later, England received a handwritten note from Hanks:

> Dear Gene,
>   Read my first letter again, throw away the second, learn, remember, be compassionate, teach.
>   And as you remember, forget and forgive.[32]

The two men continued to correspond and meet occasionally when England was in Salt Lake City, and about a year later, in November of 1969, Hanks sent a warm letter as the Englands were considering their move to St. Olaf College, affirming his personal regard despite their previous misunderstanding:

> It is easy enough to be honest and get misunderstood without having the added burden of lack of confidence in the ultimate personal sense from those presumed to love and sustain.
>
> I both love and sustain you and hope you can live long enough and stay well enough and become influential enough to do all the good things you can do with your great talents to lift and bless and strengthen. That you take a different course than I or anyone else to do that is of no great moment to me.
>
> Give Charlotte my regards and stay prayerful in this time of big difficulties and big decisions and great challenges.[33]

England also had a warm personal relationship with Neal A. Maxwell, a University of Utah political science professor and administrator and a member of the Quorum of the Twelve from 1981 to 2004, with whom England had become acquainted as a student. In 1968, while Maxwell was executive vice-president at the University of Utah, England sent Maxwell an early draft of an essay on atonement, and received this critical response:

> I am not fully persuaded . . . about whether or not it is simply "man's own sense of justice" or an eternal principle that must be satisfied. Without any extensive consideration on this point, I would guess there are some scriptures and writings which might mitigate against this view. Men's own sense of justice is highly varied. I realize you're getting at a very subtle point, but for what it's worth I am not satisfied about how well grounded your view is, but, more importantly, that the view is entirely true. I don't mean to be closed on this, merely questioning. . . . I don't mean to nit-pick, but this is an area within your article which, in my view, needs some clarification, amplification, or reconciling.[34]

In 1970, England also wrote to Maxwell about an article Maxwell had written for *The Instructor*, an official church publication for youth.

> While I am taking your time for a moment, let me also thank you for the excellent essay on the Book of Mormon in the new *Instructor*. I sometimes have trouble with your syntax when it gets a little mannered (there's the editor coming out in me), but the message is clear and powerful and can be greatly efficacious towards President Lee's suggestion quoted in the other *Instructor* article to "learn the Scriptures."[35]

Maxwell responded with gracious openness to criticism: "Help me under-stand your message about my "syntax" when it gets a little mannered. I value your editorial judgment, so don't hesitate to elaborate when you get time. I must go on learning and growing before the laws of nature make that too difficult."[36] Over many years, as Maxwell moved from Church Educational System administration into full-time clerical service, the two continued to correspond, with England sending his own writing and other things he thought the apostle might find interesting, and Maxwell occasionally passing along an article he thought noteworthy.

During the early 1990s, conflict between ecclesiastical leaders and public intellectuals in the LDS Church was intense. In September of 1993, several intellectuals and writers were subject to church discipline—excommunica-tion or a lesser punishment called disfellowshipment. The acrimony spilled into news accounts and various independent publications and forums. In 1994, England wrote to Maxwell again, proposing that perhaps a formal dialogue would be a productive way to lessen animosity and keep intrafaith disagreements from bringing negative publicity for the church. England mentioned a similar forum that had been organized to discuss interfaith issues in Salt Lake City, and suggested that

> there is need for such a regular group meeting to help resolve some of the misunderstandings and conflicts that have developed in recent years *within* the Church—and that it could succeed at least as well. If so, it would improve the tone and constructive contributions of the indepen-dent Mormon publications and forums, reduce the embarrassing and harmful displays of conflict and pain in the public media, and greatly improve the morale and effectiveness of many Mormons who wish to contribute to building the Kingdom but are feeling they are perceived and increasingly ostracized as if they were enemies. It would also, I believe, provide information that could increase the confidence of the Brethren in the intellectual and artistic communities within the Church, giving them both freedom from anxiety and incentive to use various individu-als in constructive ways.

Although no such committee was formed, the proposal is interesting as evidence of England's faith in the power of dialogue to solve even the most intractable problems. England closes the letter by noting, approvingly, that the First Presidency had made a public statement about progress in the

Israeli-Palestinian peace process, and declaring, optimistically, that "the troubling 'oppositions' within the Church are not more difficult than those in the Middle East."[37]

The Limits of Dialogue

In contrast to England's relationships with Hanks and Maxwell, which evince good will on both sides, despite disagreement, England's most famous correspondence—his conflict with Bruce R. McConkie about God's progression—lays bare the sometimes extreme difficulty of real dialogue between authoritative doctrinal interpretation and a lay member's earnest questions about ambiguities in the scriptural and prophetic canon. Their exchange is as important for the fissures in Mormon ecclesiology that it exposes as it is for the theological debate it fails to resolve.

In 1979, England gave a talk to the Honors Colloquium at Brigham Young University, titled "The Lord's University." In that talk, England described learning as a godlike quality, and said that the idea that God is progressing was especially appealing to him, because it meant the joy of learning could be eternal. The night before he was to speak, he received a call from Joseph Fielding McConkie, a BYU religion professor and son of Apostle Bruce R. McConkie. Joseph McConkie had read a draft copy of the talk that England planned to give, and told England that he felt sure Elder McConkie would not approve of its content. England was surprised because "[he] had been taught that doctrine all [his] life and believed it to be perfectly orthodox."[38] He invited the younger McConkie to respond after the talk, feeling that it would be instructive for students to see their professors respectfully disagreeing about a point of doctrine. In his response, McConkie insisted that his father and grandfather (Joseph Fielding Smith, a former president of the church) had taught of a God whose perfection was absolute and who could not possibly be progressing. McConkie's rhetoric was forceful: "Though I accord a man the privilege of worshipping what he may, there is a line—a boundary—a point at which he and his views are no longer welcome." Joseph concluded: "I do not see the salvation of BYU in the abandonment of absolutes, and with the prophets whose blood flows in my veins I refuse to worship at the shrine of an ignorant God."[39] England was shocked, and the incident caused a minor campus kerfuffle, but England did not make any public comments about his disagreement with Professor McConkie.

In June 1980, Bruce McConkie delivered a sermon at BYU titled "The Seven Deadly Heresies." After setting forth some preliminary axioms, McConkie began his list of heresies with the idea England had spoken of nine months earlier:

> Heresy one: There are those who say that God is progressing in knowledge and is learning new truths.
>
> This is false—utterly, totally, and completely. There is not one sliver of truth in it. It grows out of a wholly twisted and incorrect view of the King Follett Sermon and of what is meant by eternal progression.[40]

In September 1980, England wrote to McConkie. England explained to the apostle that, after hearing Joseph McConkie's response to his talk in the fall, he had been unsettled, and had done further research into the question of God's perfection and progress, and had written a new essay trying to distill his understanding of the historical teachings. He enclosed the essay and asked for McConkie's thoughts on this revision. England's tone was deferential, even meek:

> I have, this past year, carefully and prayerfully gone back over all the pertinent sources I could find and have written the enclosed paper about my findings. The key to harmonizing both God's perfection and His progression seems to me the concept developed by Brigham Young, I think from Doctrine and Covenants 93:30, that there are many spheres of existence, of different advancement (possibly involving different dimensions), and if we are talking *only* about ours certain truths and language are appropriate (such as perfection), but if we are considering spheres of existence far advanced *beyond* ours then other truths and language about God are equally appropriate (such as progression). But I recognize that I could certainly be wrong, that I could be interpreting Joseph Smith and Brigham Young and others incorrectly, or that subsequent revelation has invalidated what they said. I accept the authority of the *living* prophets and not only want to be but assume I am in full harmony with them, including, of course, with you. If not, I want to be put right.[41]

The paper England had drafted and sent to Bruce McConkie would be published much later as an article titled "Perfection and Progression: Two Complementary Ways to Talk About God." In that essay, England lays out the major sources for the notion that God is progressing, beginning with the King Follett sermon's assertion that "The first principle of truth and of the Gospel is to know of a certainty that character of God, . . . that He once was a man like one of us. . . . You have got to learn how to make yourselves God . . . and be kings and priests to God, the same as all Gods have done by going from a small capacity to a great capacity, from a small degree to another, from grace to grace . . . from exaltation to exaltation."

England continues by detailing Brigham Young's lengthy dispute with Orson Pratt, in which Pratt argued for God's absolute perfection and thus, the impossibility of God's "progression." Most of the citations England adduces from Young are centered on human beings' progression and learning, but there are also passages, like the following, in which Young clearly extends the principle of "eternal progression" (a phrase England credits Young with coining): "Some men seem as if they could learn so much and no more. They appear to be bounded in their capacity for acquiring knowledge, as Brother Orson has, in theory, bounded the capacity of God. According to his theory, God can progress no further in knowledge and power, but the God they serve is progressing eternally, and so are his children; they will increase to all eternity, if they are faithful."[42]

England also cites the fourth president of the church, Wilford Woodruff, who said in 1857 that "if there was a point where man in his progression could not proceed any further, the very idea would throw a gloom over every intelligent and reflecting mind. God himself is still increasing and progressing in knowledge, power and dominion, and will do so world without end."[43] The fifth president of the church, Lorenzo Snow, taught this doctrine in the most memorable and succinct formulation: "As Man now is, God once was: as God now is, Man may be."[44]

When Joseph Fielding McConkie invoked "the prophets whose blood flows in my veins" in his response to England's address, he was also tracing the lineage of the argument he and his father would make, that God's perfection is already absolute. In addition to being the son of Apostle McConkie, Professor McConkie was the son of Amelia Smith McConkie, the daughter of Joseph Fielding Smith, the tenth president of the church, who was the son of Joseph F. Smith, the sixth president of the church. Joseph F. Smith was the son of Hyrum Smith, the church's first patriarch who was martyred with his brother, the founding prophet Joseph Smith. Hyrum Smith had said, in 1844, "I would not serve a God that had not all wisdom and power." Hyrum Smith's belief in God's omniscience and omnipotence was common among early converts to Mormonism and is expressed both in some parts of the Book of Mormon and in the Lectures on Faith. These documents, incorporated into the canonical Doctrine and Covenants in 1835, present a much more absolute view of God's omnibenevolence, omniscience, and omnipotence in passages like the following:

> We here observe that God is the only supreme governor, and independent being, in whom all fulness and perfection dwells; who is omnipotent, omnipresent, and omniscient; without beginning of days or end of life; and that in him every good gift, and every good principle dwells; and that he is the Father of lights: In him the principle of faith dwells independently; and he is the object in whom the faith of all other rational and accountable beings centers, for life and salvation.[45]

> He is omnipotent, omnipresent, and omniscient; without beginning of days or end of life, and in him all fulness dwells.[46]

Although the Lectures on Faith were removed from the Doctrine and Covenants and are no longer considered scriptural, the ideas in the Lectures have never really disappeared from Mormon thought, and these passages seem to have been the major authoritative warrant for both McConkies' opposition to England's remarks. Joseph Fielding Smith (Bruce McConkie's father-in-law and Joseph McConkie's grandfather) reiterated this position, explicitly referencing interpretations of Joseph Smith's teachings that emphasized progression:

> It seems very strange to me that members of the Church will hold to the doctrine, "God increases in knowledge as time goes on."
> ... Where has the Lord ever revealed to us that he is lacking in knowledge? That he is still learning new truth; discovering new laws that are unknown to him? I think this kind of doctrine is very dangerous. I don't know where the Lord has ever declared such a thing. It is not contained in any revelation that I have read. Man's opinion unaided by the revelations of the Lord, does not make it so.[47]

England's paper tries to reconcile the two positions by positing that there are separate spheres of human and divine activity, and that God has perfect knowledge of the human sphere, but is also active in a different sphere in which God is progressing in knowledge. He relies on Witdsoe's *Rational Theology* for one description of how God's knowledge can be both complete in relationship to the universe in which human beings gain experience and knowledge, and still progressing in ways human beings cannot comprehend:

> The essential thing is that man has to undergo experience upon experience, to attain the desired mastery of the external universe; and that we, of this earth, are passing through an estate designed wholly for our further education.
>
> . . . If the great law of progression is accepted, *God must have been engaged from the beginning, and must now be engaged, in progressive development.* As knowledge grew into greater knowledge, by the persistent efforts of will, his recognition of universal laws became greater until he attained at last a conquest over the universe which to our finite understanding seems absolutely complete.[48]

England turns to a verse in the Doctrine and Covenants as theological warrant—"all truth is independent in that sphere in which God has placed it, to act for itself, as all intelligence also; otherwise there is no existence." England's interpretation of this verse asserts that "this passage seems to evoke a universe of coexistent (perhaps concentric or more likely hyperspatial, multidimensional) spheres of truth and intelligent activity." He cites Brigham Young's elaboration on these spheres as an example of how an absolute term like "perfection" might still allow for divine progress: "Mankind are organized to receive intelligence until they become perfect in the sphere they are appointed to fill, which is far ahead of us at present. *When we use the term perfection, it applies to man in his present condition, as well as the heavenly beings.* We are now, or may be, as perfect in our sphere as God and angels are in theirs, but the greatest intelligence in existence can continually ascend to greater heights of perfection."[49]

England acknowledges the concern of those like Joseph F. Smith, Joseph Fielding Smith, and Bruce McConkie who worry that speaking of God as progressing is diminishing or belittling. He also admits that it is fearsome to contemplate a less than entirely perfect or omniscient God. And yet, he concludes, the "absolute, changeless, impassive, and thus necessarily impersonal God of traditional Christianity and of the philosophers" is still more frightening to him.

England was in London leading a study abroad program when McConkie replied to his letter and the draft essay in February 1981, so it was months before England actually read the letter (dated 19 February 1981), although he heard about it from friends who had seen a copy that was circulating on BYU's campus in Provo. To call McConkie's response "blistering" would be understating the matter by quite a bit. McConkie said he was "extending . . . the hand of fellowship," but reminded England that he also held over him "at the same time, the scepter of judgment." He recapitulated the major points of his "Seven Deadly Heresies" talk, refuting the idea that God could possibly be continuing to learn and progress. He continued by quoting another of his own talks:

> There are even those who champion the almost unbelievable theory that God is an Eternal Student enrolled in the University of the Universe where he is busily engaged in learning new truths and amassing new and strange knowledge that he never knew before.
>
> How belittling it is—it borders on blasphemy—to demean the Lord God Omnipotent by saying . . . that he is ever learning but never able to come to a knowledge of all truth.[50]

Perhaps the most surprising part of the letter is McConkie's dismissal of the quotations from Brigham Young. He writes:

> Prophets are men and they make mistakes. Sometimes they err in doctrine. This is one of the reasons the Lord has given us the Standard Works.[51] They become the standards and rules that govern where doctrine and philosophy are concerned. . . . Sometimes a prophet gives personal views which are not endorsed and approved by the Lord.
>
> . . .
>
> Yes, Brigham Young did say some things about God progressing in knowledge and understanding, but again, be it known, that Brigham Young taught, emphatically and plainly, that God knows all things and has all power[,] meaning in the infinite, eternal, and ultimate and absolute sense of the word. Again, the issue is, which Brigham Young shall we believe? . . . As for me and my house, we will have the good sense to choose between the divergent teachings of the same man and come up with those that accord with what God has set forth in his eternal plan of salvation.

McConkie devotes the final three pages of the nine-page letter to emphasizing his authority to declare doctrine. He cites Ephesians as scriptural warrant for his responsibility and prerogative to ensure that church members are not "tossed to and fro, and carried about with every wind of doctrine." "This means," he writes, " . . . that it is my province to teach to the Church what the doctrine is. It is your province to echo what I say or to remain silent." McConkie does not claim infallibility; he is careful to acknowledge the possibility that he might make a mistake, but the consequences of his mistakes and England's mistakes, he argues, are different: "If I err, that is my problem; but in your case if you single out some of these things and make them the center of your philosophy, and end up being wrong, you will lose your soul."

While McConkie acknowledges that a prophet could be mistaken, and even repeats a quotation of Joseph Smith that seems to create some possibility of faithful dissent—"a prophet is not always a prophet, only when he is acting as such"—he immediately forecloses that possibility with the strenuous assertion of his own prerogative to declare doctrine. The method he suggests for discerning when a prophet is "acting as such" is harmonizing prophetic pronouncements with scripture, which could be a liberalizing approach if laypersons were encouraged to undertake it. However, McConkie seems to suggest that his understanding of scripture supersedes England's. His confidence reflects both his personality and, more importantly, a shift in Mormon ecclesiology.

The intensity of McConkie's response is somewhat startling in the context of even a significant disagreement about the nature of God. His conflict with England may have been especially fraught because it was standing in for larger issues with which the church was grappling as the twentieth century entered its latter decades. The question of how doctrine was to be promulgated had never been simple for Mormons. Joseph Smith's revelations were dictated through many amanuenses, his sermons were recorded by various scribes, and interpretations of his teachings were written and published by many people, sometimes authorized and sometimes not. Even the hymnal was contested—at times there were as many as five or six different sets of songs in use in Mormon congregations. By the time leaders began trying to establish more officially regulated channels for publishing in the early years of the twentieth century, various auxiliaries—the Sunday School, and organizations for women, youth, children—were all publishing their own manuals, magazines, and newspapers. All contained lessons that were regarded as at least quasi-official teachings of the church. Folk doctrines proliferated, as did older teachings that were falling out of favor but had not been officially disavowed.

And it was not only folk doctrine that caused problems. In fact, some of the other "Deadly Heresies" McConkie was denouncing at the same time as his conflict with England were teachings of past presidents of the church. This was not mere hubris on McConkie's part—in a church committed to the possibility of ongoing revelation, authoritative teachings of the past must be subject to revision, and there have been few clearly articulated rules within Mormonism about how such revision may proceed.

Liberal-leaning Mormons like to adduce quotations from early prophets that seem to license broad theological conjecture. On one occasion, Joseph Smith is reported to have defended a man named Pelatiah Brown who was accused of preaching false doctrine, saying, "I did not like the old man being called up for erring in doctrine. It looks too much like the Methodist, and not like the Latter-day Saints. Methodists have creeds which a man must believe or be asked out of their church. I want the liberty of thinking and believing as I please. It feels so good not to be trammelled. It does not prove that a man is not a good man because he errs in doctrine."[52]

Yet on another occasion, a member of the church named Hiram Page claimed to have a seer stone like Smith's and to be receiving revelation. Smith dispatched his assistant Oliver Cowdery to go and persuade Page that these revelations were from the devil, and get Page to declare that Smith was the only authorized revelator for the church.

Smith's successor, Brigham Young, had an authoritarian style of governing the church and little patience for dissent, but he also insisted that his followers should not "have so much confidence in their leaders that they will not inquire for themselves of God whether they are led by him." He urged them to avoid "reckless confidence" and to find out, "by the whispering of the Spirit of God to themselves, whether their leaders are walking in the path the Lord dictates, or not."[53]

Thus, from the beginning, one of the great unresolved tensions of Mormonism was exactly over whether the kind of dialogic engagement England sought was licit, or whether the need for true ecclesiastical authority required a hierarchical approach in which truth was determined by those at the top and disseminated to the members below. As they do with the questions of God's finitude and progression, Mormons who consider themselves perfectly orthodox believe, in varying proportions, that ecclesiastical authority confers doctrinal authority to which members are bound to defer, *and* that authorities can be mistaken in doctrinal interpretation, *and* that individual Saints are allowed or even obliged to work out doctrinal understanding using their God-given intellect and personal inspiration. Even apostles differ in their assertion of doctrinal authority. In contrast to McConkie's absolutism, consider this letter from Apostle Neal A. Maxwell to a colleague of England's at the University of Utah Institute of Religion, on another perennially thorny issue in Mormon theology, the question of whether human beings can progress between kingdoms in the afterlife.[54] Maxwell responds to the question in a way an academic might expect, with a willingness to admit ignorance and a tolerance for ambiguity:

> My own reaction is fairly simple; the earlier communications of the Presidency indicate that some of the brethren have held post-resurrection progress a possibility, while others have taken an opposite view, and that the newly-cited reference (D&C 76:112) simply indicates what must be one boundary line, namely, that those who inherit the telestial glory cannot come "worlds without end" where God and Christ dwell. In other words, we know only so much about this matter beyond which anything is speculative, but that verse sounds pretty controlling to me with regard to telestial beings.
>
> I realize you and I are comfortable holding this kind of matter in abeyance until the Lord gives us more information, whereas some of our youth are anxious to nail things down in a definitive way that is simply not possible.[55]

All of these questions about how doctrine should be authoritatively articulated became more pressing as the church expanded. England's correspondence with General Authorities is a valuable record of the widely varied ways in which Mormonism's ecclesiastical structure adapted (and didn't) to the stresses of a rapidly growing and diversifying laity. England's concerns were largely those of well-educated American Mormons with generational ties to the church, or at least years'-long experience as church members, while the pressing concerns of General Authorities were increasingly with translating the most basic teachings of the church into the languages and cultures of areas where the church was expanding—a notable feature of England's correspondence with General Authorities is the number of times they apologize for a delayed response due to travel.

The Quorum of the Twelve was initially designated as a missionary body. Section 107 of the Doctrine and Covenants, recorded in 1835, sets out their role: "The traveling councilors are called to be the Twelve Apostles, or special witnesses of the name of Christ in all the world—thus differing from other officers in the church in the duties of their calling." While their role had shifted gradually since Joseph Smith's death, it changed quite dramatically in the mid- to late twentieth century, in response to the growth of the church and to the internal dynamics of the Quorum. As the church grew in the 1950s and 1960s, efforts to streamline its administration become urgent. Rather than traveling missionaries and pastors, apostles became part of a committee structure set up to govern various functions of the church and their job descriptions began to encompass more administrative tasks and fewer pastoral ones. Coincidentally, several presidents of the church during this time (Heber J. Grant, George Albert Smith, and Joseph Fielding Smith) were in ill health and unable to lead as vigorously as their counselors and the leadership of the Quorum of the Twelve, which had the effect of augmenting the Quorum's influence.

Apostle Harold B. Lee was assigned to chair the Correlation Committee in 1960 with the task of bringing the various programs and auxiliaries of the church under centralized control. Lee's program for achieving this goal involved organizing the Quorum of the Twelve into various committees overseeing missionary work, the construction and operating of temples, the development of curricula, official church publications, and so forth. Consolidating all of these programs under the leadership of the Quorum of the Twelve gave the body more direct and specific control over all aspects of Mormon life.[56] Although they still preached sermons when they traveled, much of the apostles' time was spent training new leaders in how to run units of the church.

Beginning in the 1930s, the educational background of the Quorum of the Twelve changed, as well. The men appointed as apostles in the 1940s and 1950s were much more likely to have backgrounds in business or law than in academia. Perhaps coincidentally, they also tended to be more conservative theologically than those who served in the early part of the twentieth century. Sociologist Armand Mauss, in describing the effect of this gradual change, observes that people with different training and careers think about problems differently, and those educated in business administration, engineering, and law are likely to approach problems, including church problems, in ways that are more pragmatic and results-oriented than the way academics might engage with them, focusing on analysis and careful process. The result of the changing composition of the highest bodies of church leadership thus inevitably changed both the kinds of problems leaders were attuned to and the perception of how church leaders should think about them:

> The near-total disappearance of leaders with the more scientific or schol-arly orientation from the topmost ranks of the church leadership thus implies that with the passage of time there would be a corresponding diminution within that leadership of their collective capacity to accom-modate diversity, relativity, or ambiguity in church policies or programs, to say nothing of doctrines. Such a leadership would naturally be increas-ingly hospitable to proposals for greater correlation, centralization, and other forms of retrenchment in the face of growing ambiguity about what assimilated Mormonism really "stands for" in the modern world.[57]

Whether or not Mauss's conjecture about the intellectual proclivities of current apostles is correct, the effect of the increasing administrative burden borne by members of the Quorum of the Twelve and First Presidency seems to be that these theological disputes are pushed out of the hierarchy. It is difficult to imagine apostles now writing ten-page letters to laypeople about almost anything. Indeed, current church policy is for letters from church members addressed to apostles about doctrinal matters to be referred to the letter-writer's local leaders. General Conference sermons and official curricula seem heavily weighted toward the ethical and practical implica-tions of Mormon ideas that have been simplified to meet the needs of a rapidly expanding organization with many converts to assimilate and a shrinking cohort of lifelong members who might be interested in exploring a wider range of Mormonism's theological questions. While it is impossible to know how much theological debate happens now among members of the Quorum of the Twelve, an increased emphasis on the unanimity among the Brethren means that apostles no longer have public arguments about theology. Without models for disagreement, members tend to conclude that disagreement is undesirable or even forbidden.

These kinds of conflicts now occur almost exclusively in unofficial fo-rums and on the internet, and at lower levels of institutional authority than the Quorum of the Twelve. While there are still Mormons who would like to see England's expansive view of Mormonism become more wide-spread, England's experience suggests that their hopes for institutional adjustment will not be realized by direct appeal to General Authorities. The process of doctrinal adaptation has become more diffuse in the twenty-first century—the range of Latter-day Saints' experience, doctrinal literacy, and theological interest is much wider than it was at mid-twentieth century; the push for doctrinal standardization, therefore, no longer seems apt. However, contrary to Mauss's prediction that the pragmatic bent of LDS leadership would result in "a . . . diminution within that leadership of their collective capacity to accommodate diversity, relativity, or ambiguity in church policies or programs, to say nothing of doctrines," the response to the changing and increasingly diverse needs of church membership seems to be an *increase* in flexibility and tolerance for varied viewpoints and open-ended doctrinal discussion. At the same time as the church introduced a slim new volume intended to provide the entire authoritative curriculum for all of the church's programs, leaders also encouraged members to embrace "home-centered, church-supported" religious learning, study in families and small groups. This marks a significant contrast to the later years of England's life, when "study groups" were discouraged and members were enjoined not to heed "alternate voices" that might discuss doctrine outside of official church forums.[58]

Throughout his career, England's commitment to dialogue seemed to multiply and amplify such "alternate voices." Besides the journal *Dialogue*, which is still published quarterly more than fifty years after its founding and now has a web presence and regular podcasts, England was instrumental in the founding of the Association for Mormon Letters, which has sponsored varied publications and an annual meeting since 1976. He encouraged the founders of *Sunstone* magazine and regularly published in its pages and participated in its annual symposia. England encouraged a small group of Mormon feminists to guest edit an issue of *Dialogue* and cheered them on as they established *Exponent II*, which continues quarterly publication and also hosts an annual gathering to discuss Mormon doctrine and practice in relation to women's concerns. England's establishment of the Mormon studies program at Utah Valley University was a harbinger of the flowering of Mormon studies in the academy—the establishment of chaired professorships in Mormon studies at Claremont Graduate University, the University of Virginia, Utah State University (with Mormon studies programs at the University of Utah, Utah Valley University, the University of Southern California, and the Graduate Theological Union) as well as the proliferation of conferences devoted to Mormon topics in a wide range of disciplines.

With the notable exception of the Mormon History Association's conference, in which many employees of the church's Historical Department and Church History Library participate, most of these conferences occur without official participation, sponsorship, or blessing or condemnation. The church itself has undertaken significant scholarly projects, including a massive documentary history project to publish papers related to Joseph Smith's life and work. The Church Historical Department moved from the Church Office Building to a large, new facility in 2007, broadening the accessibility of records and making a great deal of archival material open to scholars and the general public for the first time. The sheer number of scholars discussing Mormonism, and the variety of their commitments to Mormon institutions, make doctrinal policing impossible, even if someone from the central hierarchy were inclined to do it. Dialogue about Mormon ideas, Mormon culture, and Mormon theology has blossomed in ways that England could not have foreseen, but would surely have celebrated.

With the benefit of twenty years of hindsight, it seems that perhaps the doctrinal reconciliation England sought with McConkie was unnecessary—they were living on the hinge between correlation and its unwinding. Where the story of Mormonism in the twentieth century was one of streamlining and centralization, the story of Mormonism in the early twenty-first century is the gradual simplification of doctrinal instruction and the shrinking of unified curricula. Rather than developing a mechanism for articulating authoritative doctrine in disputed areas, the church has evolved to require assent to ever fewer doctrinal propositions, marking the boundaries of community instead by behavior (a dietary code, tithe-paying, premarital abstinence from sex and heterosexual monogamy, church attendance, etc.) and active participation in church programs. England's assertion that "the Church is as true as the gospel" turns out to be right in ways he could not have predicted.

CHAPTER 4

Reconciliation and Atonement

> When I applied [for a professorship at BYU], some on the
> hiring committee rejoiced that an obviously liberal founder
> of *Dialogue* was coming to shake up the administration and
> conservative student body. . . . Then, when it turned out I was
> really a conservative, who had prayer in classes and believed
> the Church is as true as the gospel, a provincial who offered
> a book on Brigham Young as part of my scholarship when
> I applied for promotion and who wanted the department to
> teach more of our own Mormon heritage and culture through
> Mormon literature, I was attacked and punished. Now, twenty
> years later, I find myself labeled a liberal, publicly attacked
> and privately punished, not for violating the academic freedom
> document prescriptions against criticizing Church leaders or
> opposing Church doctrine, but for violating cultural taboos
> that are mistakenly made into religious issues.
>
> Eugene England, "'No Cause, No Cause':
> An Essay toward Reconciliation"

England uses "liberal" and "conservative" often, and sometimes rather imprecisely. It will be helpful to tease out the various contexts in which England employed that terminology. Chapter 3 discussed strains of Mormon theology that could be considered liberal and conservative, at least with respect to each other. In this chapter, I will consider cultural and political contexts in which Mormons can be divided (always imperfectly, of course), and have divided themselves, into categories labeled liberal and conservative, and how Eugene England tried to construct space for liberal and conservative ideas to exist in productive tension rather than enmity with each other.

Just as the theological conflicts between Mormon "liberals" and "conservatives" were already beginning to recede toward the end of England's life, cultural and political divisions between liberals and conservatives were becoming as entrenched among Mormons as among Americans broadly. Some Mormons were increasingly making common cause with the "religious right," despite theological differences that had animated the anti-cult movement's targeting of Mormonism in the late 1970s and 1980s. Although England was involved in liberal political movements, he inherited the Depression-era disdain for FDR from his father and his Idaho neighbors, and remained a registered Republican for most of his life, voting twice for Richard Nixon and twice for Ronald Reagan.[1] His views became more liberal starting in graduate school, but he did not switch parties. His writings on politics were always grounded in Mormon ideas, and he divided the world not between Democrats and Republicans, but between Mormons and non-Mormons. In an essay about visiting Washington, DC, for the dedication of the temple there, for instance, England recalled a conversation with Mary Bradford (a friend, and one of his successors as editor of *Dialogue*), who thought that Mormons in the capital "face some special problems in the corridors of power. She felt that basic Mormon ideals and conditioning made them especially vulnerable, particularly naive and reticent, incapable of certain instincts and possibilities of action demanded in the heady infighting of the big government–big business complexes." England's response seems like a dramatic intensification of the divide Bradford was suggesting:

> Perhaps she is right; Christ talked of the Children of Darkness being wiser in some things than the Children of Light. The Byzantine depths revealed by Watergate are perhaps, and perhaps we can rejoice at it, beyond our fathoming; if indeed the Elders of Israel are to save the Constitution they may perhaps best do it indirectly, or at least at lower levels of power, by in some sense coming out of Babylon and avoiding both her sins and her plagues.[2]

While England must be thinking here of Luke 16:8 ("for the children of this world are in their generation wiser than the children of light"), the words he chooses might be unconsciously borrowed from Reinhold Niebuhr's 1944 book, *The Children of Light and the Children of Darkness*. Niebuhr would have rejected England's conception of a finite, progressing God, and certainly would have criticized some of his more optimistic liberal political ideals, but Niebuhr's insistence on action, dialogic critique, and the necessary and irresolvable contradictions of Christian discipleship would be quite compatible with the principles that seem to guide England's thought. England's wrestling with the question of the self in religious community, his insistence that neither absolute fealty to authority nor absolute defer- ence to individual conscience can create a virtuous society would resonate with Niebuhr's conclusion that both groups and individuals are capable of "idolatrous self-worship," and that morality requires a precarious balance between them: "The problem of the individual and the community cannot be solved at all if the height is not achieved where the sovereign source and end of both individual and communal existence are discerned, and where the limits are set against the idolatrous self-worship of both individuals and communities."[3] Like Niebuhr, England rejects the notion that believ- ers should relegate politics to the realm of the secular. In an essay about Mormons and Watergate, England asserts that Mormon beliefs about the nature of God and the universe ought to influence Mormon political par- ticipation. Because Mormon teachings describe a universe that is organized according to rational and therefore discoverable natural laws, rather than "arbitrarily *willed* by a sovereign and inscrutable God and thus beyond man's understanding," England insists that Mormons ought to have an extraordinary commitment to knowable truth:

> The laws of goodness and truth are *natural*, inherent in the very nature of things which have always existed, "co-eternal" with God and man (and physical laws) and "irrevocable"—and thus knowable through human experience and analysis as well as through revelation. Truth is something that can and should be *discovered* and that then directly demands and merits our loyalty, not something we wait for some authority to decide for us.
>
> . . . The truth about what is evil, harmful, unlawful, does not change when it is done in the service of high authority or high-sounding pur- pose—like "national security." We believe that we are accountable not just to leaders, but to the universe, to the nature of things; and leaders are accountable to the universe too. We believe that even God is God because He knows the nature of the universe and obeys.[4]

And in England's most directly political essay, "Why Some Utah Mormons Should Become Democrats," he exhibits a distinctly Niebuhrian pragma- tism and willingness to make expedient compromises. In *The Children of Light and the Children of Darkness*, Niebuhr sketches three postures that believers might take in politics—1) a religious approach which seeks to eliminate religious diversity and restore an original unity; 2) a secular approach which treats religion as irrelevant; and 3) "a religious approach which seeks to maintain religious vitality within the conditions of religious diversity." Niebuhr described America (in the 1940s) as "partially secularized," "favoring religious toleration because it does not regard the religious convictions which create religious differences in the community as significant."[5]

Many Mormon discussions of political participation, both in England's time and much earlier, seem to accept the idea that an explicitly secular state is the best mechanism for protecting Mormons' right to act as believing individuals. This, in Niebuhr's view, is naïve and doomed to failure:

> The fact is that a theory of democratic toleration which enjoins provisional freedom for all religions in the hope that the bourgeois climate of opinion will gradually dissipate all religious convictions except the secularized bourgeois versions of them, is a typical fruit of the illusions of modern "children of light." They expect modern society to achieve an essential uniformity through the common convictions of "men of good-will" who have been enlightened by modern liberal education.[6]

Instead, Niebuhr suggests, "the children of light" should act in more calculated ways, recognizing that the pure expression of their ideals cannot succeed. "The achievement of communal harmony on the basis of secularism means the sacrifice of religious profundity as the price of a tolerable communal accord. It is a dangerous sacrifice; but it would be well for religious devotees who criticize secularism to recognize that it has sometimes been a necessary one."[7] England's treatment is subtler in its appreciation of the role of religious believers *as a community*, and suggests exactly the sort of clear-eyed compromise Niebuhr calls a necessary sacrifice. England begins by recounting an episode in Huntsville, Utah, in 1891, when, according to local lore, church leaders went door-to-door to assign households to the Republican and Democratic parties in equal numbers. Because a Republican president, Benjamin Harrison, had just presided over a coercive effort to force Utah Mormons to abandon the practice of polygamy, church leaders feared that most Mormons would want to become Democrats. They feared that, in turn, non-Mormons in Utah would all become Republicans, thus hardening political divisions between Mormons and "Gentiles" and diluting the ability of Mormons to influence policy by electing legislators in both parties, who could then form coalitions on issues of importance to Latter-day Saints. This view, says England, "shows better insight into the nature and value of political parties than that of many Mormons today, mostly Republicans, who believe the Truth resides with their party and that salvation will come with its supremacy." In 1988, when he published the essay, it was still possible to say that Democrats were "a steadily dwindling minority" in Utah, and it was still possible for England to urge that some Republicans should become Democrats. "I believe some Utah Mormons should become Democrats for precisely the same reason the First Presidency encouraged some to become Republicans in 1891: 'The more evenly balanced the parties become the safer it will be for us in the security of our liberties; and . . . our influence for good will be far greater than it possibly could be were either party overwhelmingly in the majority.'" Note that, in the schema England suggests, it is the religious collective that asks the individual to subvert her voting preference for the sake of preserving a moral political process. The religious minority thus influences the majority by safeguarding its role in the process, rather than directly asserting its moral preference. England warned that Mormons were becoming intent on using the legislative process to prohibit particular practices they regarded as immoral, rather than writing laws that would preserve maximum freedom for individual belief and practice in moral matters. England notes that Mormons (in the 1980s) had begun making common cause with Republicans in such efforts. He suggests that Mormons' tendency toward utopian thinking and history of living in communities bounded by strict behavioral norms make them blind to the dangers of the Republican project to Mormons as a minority: "[The] effort by Republicans to do God's work for him, to use the power of the state to do what only churches and other non-coercive social and cultural forces should ever try to do, once led the party into one of the most outrageous intrusions upon human rights in American history, . . . the anti-polygamy crusade against the Mormons."[8] Despite his frequent ambivalence about individual submission to authority in the church, England suggests that "it might be good for our Church leaders to encourage us to do some . . . old-fashioned dividing of congregations or at least some quiet assignments to even-numbered stake presidents and bishops." England feared that if a supermajority of Mormons remained Republican, religion and politics would become ever more entangled in Utah, and that partisan division would reinforce divisions between Mormons and non-Mormons.[9]

England had identified the trend correctly. In the 2000 presidential election, 67 percent of Utah voters voted for the Republican nominee, and in 2004, that number rose to 72 percent. Utah voters are, of course, not all Mormon, but Mormon voters are still a significant majority. In the United States, 65 percent of Latter-day Saints identify as Republicans or lean toward the Republican party, and 60 percent self-identify as politically "conservative," while only 6 percent identify as "liberal." England's concern about Utah politics coming to pit exclusively Republican Mormons against Democratic non-Mormons is also coming to pass, as Utah's booming economy attracts immigrants from other states and Mormons become a minority in a few parts of Utah. At the end of his life, England lamented that Mormons were joining with Evangelical Christians in social and political activities that he feared would divide the Saints:

> A call for greater "cooperation" between Evangelicals and Mormons in social and political action . . . seems to me to translate into active social conservativism, which in recent times has meant, in my judgment, mainly negative and divisive activities: pro-family through narrowing our definition of family, anti-pornography through censorship, anti-abortion through restricting choice, anti-gay rights, anti-affirmative action, anti-gun control. It's certainly fine for Mormons to choose to engage in such activities, but it is a tragedy that, increasingly, those are made to appear as the official and only appropriate forms of political action for Mormons.[10]

Cultural "Conservatives" and "Liberals"

These political divisions substantially carry over into Mormon culture, but describing "conservative" and "liberal" Mormons is not quite as simple as checking voter registrations. England observed on many occasions that "conservative" and "liberal" ought to be essentially neutral shorthand for different approaches to questions about culture and public policy. He insisted that they should not be terms by which Mormons categorized and judged each other, because Mormon teachings encompass both liberal elements—an expansive and optimistic view of human nature, an open canon—and conservative tendencies—strict codes of personal behavior and a culture of intense loyalty to leaders.

The loyalty and deference to leaders that England both championed and chafed at was always a significant facet of Mormon culture, but its contours changed substantially during England's life. England recalled the visit of an apostle to his stake conference as a formative experience of his youth. Such gatherings would have included perhaps a thousand people. Now it is more common for apostles to visit groups of several thousand Saints in rented arenas. Most members' experience of General Authorities is via television. This inevitably creates a kind of institutional celebrity that did not exist when England was a young man, and it changes the way that members of the church think and speak about leaders in the central church hierarchy. A sort of performative public deference to authority has become a more significant cultural expectation as the General Authorities have become more distant from the growing membership of the church. Not only disagreement with church leaders, but also speaking of them too casually or familiarly—referring to them without their titles or even leaving out the middle initials that are traditionally included in referring to them—is sometimes interpreted as evidence that the speaker is not properly orthodox. Other issues of style—dress (dresses for women and suits and white shirts for men are still expected for Sunday meetings), grooming (facial hair is still prohibited for both professors and students at BYU, for instance, presumably a relic of anxiety about "hippies" in the 1960s and early 1970s), even linguistic tics (the use of archaic pronouns in prayers and the deployment of faddish phrases like "tender mercies" from General Authorities' sermons)—often demarcate "liberal" and "conservative" believers.[11] Cultural shibboleths have acquired new significance as requirements for doctrinal orthodoxy have receded.

England grappled with these changes, sometimes theoretically and sometimes very concretely in his religious and professional life. Finding the proper balance of "the courage to be as oneself" and "the courage to be as a part," to borrow Paul Tillich's terminology, was a struggle throughout his life and career. Although England experienced and wrote of these difficulties in Mormon terms, they were salient issues in the larger American culture as well. Questions about the role of the individual, and tensions between the human need to belong and the need for self-expression had been in the zeitgeist since (at least) England's time in graduate school. In *The Organization Man* (published in 1956, but reprinted throughout the

1960s, with a new edition produced as recently as 2002), for instance, William Whyte laid out essentially the same problems that England describes in Mormonism—both the human need to belong and the institutional needs of large organizations were in conflict with the development and expression of individual agency and integrity. Whyte, too, suggested that a greater tolerance for the tensions involved, rather than the resolution of them in favor of "belongingness" would be salutary:

> There is always the common thread that a man must belong and that he must be unhappy if he does not belong rather completely. The idea that conflicting allegiances safeguard him as well as abrade him is sloughed over, and for the people who must endure the tensions of independence there is no condolence; only the message that the tensions are sickness— either in themselves or in society. It does not make any difference whether the Good Society is to be represented by a union or by a corporation or by a church, it is to be a society unified and purged of conflict.
>
> To turn about and preach that conflicting allegiances are absolute virtues is not justified either. But at this particular time the function they perform in the maintenance of individual freedom is worthy of more respect.[12]

It was not only sociologists and psychologists who were interested in these questions. Theological engagement with problems of the individual in society was also high. Paul Tillich's 1952 monograph *The Courage to Be* sold widely; Tillich became popular and influential enough to appear on multiple covers of *Time* magazine over two decades. *The Courage to Be* devotes several chapters to questions about the relationship of the individual to the group. Tillich asserts that courage is required both to be as an individual and to be as a part of a larger whole: the courage to be is essentially always the courage to be as a part and the courage to be as oneself, in interdependence.[13]

England transposed these questions and insights into a Mormon context. Several essays in England's first published collection of essays *Dialogues with Myself* wrestle in one way or another with the paradoxical relationship between individual integrity and loyal obedience. In "Obedience, Integrity, and the Paradox of Selfhood," England articulates the paradox in the context of belonging to a church that values group cohesion and loyalty: "The tension between the conflicting values of individual integrity on the one hand and on the other obedience to a God we believe is acting through his servants, a tension which exists at all levels of the Church and from earliest times, is a tension that should *not* be resolved in favor of one or the other of those conflicting values."[14]

In this essay and throughout his work, England frequently valorizes men[15] who recognize the problem of authority, but continue to willingly submit. He notes the example of B. H. Roberts, who had a long-running disagreement with Joseph F. Smith, a member of the First Presidency, stemming from Roberts's involvement in Democratic politics. Roberts felt that he had lost a congressional election because of Smith's interference, and he was temporarily suspended from the Presidency of the Seventy (along with Moses Thatcher, who was suspended from the Quorum of the Twelve) after refusing to accept a First Presidency mandate against apostles holding political office while serving in the Quorum, a decree which Roberts felt was motivated by partisanship. Unlike Thatcher, who would not submit and was permanently removed from the Quorum and became estranged from the church, Roberts ultimately changed his mind, agreed to the prohibition, and publicly confessed that he had been mistaken in his earlier opposition.

England also cites the example of Orson Pratt, whose brilliant and prolific writing on doctrinal matters led him into decades-long disagreements with Brigham Young. On at least two occasions, Young required Pratt to issue public retractions of his teachings, and then asked Pratt to submit his writing and his sermons for approval before publishing or delivering them. In 1868, Pratt and Young again had a strong disagreement. This time, Pratt did not wait to be censured or asked to retract his opinions. He wrote a penitent letter to Young, asking for forgiveness for his stubbornness and for "foolishly trying to justify [him]self in advocating ideas, opposed to those which have been introduced by the highest authorities of the Church, and adopted by the Saints." England cites this example as a "heroic though painful transcendence of the paradox" of obedience and integrity.

As an example of submission to the authority of the collective with disastrous results, however, England relates the case of John D. Lee, a rancher and member of the Territorial Legislature from Iron County in southern Utah, who played a key part in the September 1857 massacre of about one hundred members of the Baker-Fancher party, a group of emigrants traveling from Arkansas to California. The Mormon settlers of the area, vigilant in the ongoing conflict with the American federal government, and aroused by false rumors that members of the emigrant party had been present when several Mormons were killed at Haun's Mill, Missouri, dispatched a militia to confront the members of the Baker-Fancher wagon train. Lee at first outspokenly opposed the plan, but later concluded that he must lay aside his "weakness and humanity and [become] an instrument in the hands of [his] superiors and leaders." He was sent to the Fancher camp to falsely promise the train safe passage and convince them to give up their arms. The militia then attacked the unarmed emigrants and killed all but the youngest children. Lee was the only person ever tried and convicted for his role in the massacre, and he was executed by firing squad in 1877. England insists on the moral complexity of Lee's decision, and the similar dilemmas that conscientious believers in prophetic leadership must confront:

> It will just not do to dismiss John D. Lee as a religious fanatic, victimized by the conditioning of his Mormonism toward blind obedience. To do so is to demean the genuine paradox, the tragic complexity, of his situation; it is to come down too easily on the side of integrity to self, of inner conviction of moral right, over obedience to those one firmly believes—*also* on the basis of inner conviction—are his leaders on the path of salvation.[16]

In several other essays, England further examines the dilemmas of the individual in an authoritative church in the example of Levi Savage Jr. Savage converted to Mormonism in 1846, and went west to Utah with the earliest groups of Mormon pioneers. In 1852, he was sent on a series of missionary journeys. He set out for Siam, first traveling west through Las Vegas to Los Angeles and San Francisco. He sailed to Calcutta, India, but was unable to reach Siam because of a civil war, and so spent two-and-a-half years in Rangoon and Moulmein, Burma. He returned to the United States in 1856, landing in Boston, and then made his way to Winter Quarters, Nebraska, where he encountered a group of English Mormons preparing to make the journey to Utah. However, the English group was not prepared to leave Winter Quarters until August, which Savage knew was far too late in the season to begin the trek. Having seen early winters on the plains and in the Rockies, Savage warned that they ought to wait until spring rather than risk being trapped by early snow and bitter cold. Church leaders overruled his objections and promised that God would protect the travelers. Franklin Richards publicly rebuked Savage for his lack of faith. Savage did not relent in his warning, but finally declared, "Brethren and sisters, what I have said I know to be true; but, seeing you are to go forward, I will go with you, will help you all I can, will work with you, will rest with you, will suffer with you, and if necessary, I will die with you. May God in His mercy bless and preserve us."[17]

Savage, of course, was right about the dangers of setting out that late in the year. The handcart companies, led by Edward Martin and James Willie, were overtaken by the mountain winter and suffered grievously—of 900 members of the companies that left Winter Quarters after Savage's warning, 210 died, and many more suffered frostbite and starvation. Ultimately, they were rescued after Franklin D. Richards, returning from a mission, passed them and rode ahead (with his lighter, better-equipped wagon and horses) to Salt Lake to bring back supplies and help.

To appreciate England's use of this history, it is important to know that the misfortunes of the Martin and Willie handcart companies are often adduced as an example of stalwart obedience and great faith. Stories of the handcart pioneers' suffering and faithfulness are frequently recounted in Mormon sermons, including General Conference sermons by apostles and church presidents. England's valorization of reason and dissent *as well as* obedience reflects his constant desire to find reconciliation between religious values that seem to be in tension with each other.

As an example of his own contemporaries facing this sort of paradox, England outlines the dilemma of Latter-day Saints troubled by the denial of priesthood and temple rituals to Black members of the church for many decades. Those who objected to the proscriptions but remained practicing church members had to set aside their moral, social, and political convictions, submit to the disapproval of friends and colleagues, and accept (or at least listen to) sermons that violated their moral reasoning and their understanding of scriptural teachings about the equality and divinity of all human beings.

England had written publicly about the priesthood and temple ban for over a decade before the policies related to Black members of the church changed in 1978. Although England hoped for the policy to change, he believed that it must have been inspired if multiple prophets had maintained the policy. He condemned those who resolved the paradox by exiting the church: "those . . . failed who emotionally opted for their own personal vision, rejected the authority of the Church and loyalty to their community, and blamed Brigham

Young or the current prophet or other supposedly racist Mormons, never themselves." However, he also condemns those who merely obeyed: "Those who failed the test, I believe, are those who thoughtlessly obeyed, even rationalizing the mystery away by finding some way to blame the blacks because of their supposed lineage or pre-existent mistakes."[18] He celebrated the example of Apostle Hugh Brown, who urged members to pray to discover and have the courage to root out racism in themselves, so that they would be ready when the policy changed. England distinguishes this introspective loyalty from "thoughtless obedience," insisting that the challenge membership in a group poses to individual integrity can be resisted without exalting individual conscience to an idol or allowing the "absolutely necessary civilized forms" of the group to become tyrannical.[19]

England's conflicting commitments to upholding the actions of church leaders he believed to be inspired and to his own moral intuition against racism leads him into a very complicated analysis. He distinguishes between the policy itself, which he believed was divinely revealed, and the racist rationales for that policy offered by church leaders and members, which he believed were not divinely inspired. He suggests that the peculiar history of the United States' practice of slavery had resulted in deeply rooted prejudices that would have made it impossible for a fully integrated and structurally equitable church to avoid schism. He concludes that the priesthood was withheld from Black Latter-day Saint men not because they did not deserve to be ordained, but because white people would not have been able to accept those ordinations—a merciful God allowed the church to live by a lower law to preserve at least the possibility of church membership for Black people until white people were prepared to attempt to live the higher law of equality:

> Given its particular nature, the restored Church could not, during the period of slavery and its bitter heritage when American blacks and whites could not relate as equals, ease the transition by segregating congregations or keeping blacks out of leadership and priesthood functions through educational requirements, etc. . . . Until quite recently, giving blacks the priesthood would have been greatly destructive to the Church because of white reaction and thus not a blessing to blacks.[20]

The troubling instrumentalism of England's position on the racist priesthood ban suggests the limits of the effort to live within the paradox rather than resolving it—the individual conscience is salved and group cohesion is maintained, but sometimes without meaningfully addressing the ethical issues that produced the conflict between the individual and the group in the first place.

In all of the cases England adduces as examples of the paradoxes involved in individuals' relationship to a church community, it at least appears that individual integrity was sacrificed for the sake of obedience to authority. And there are, strikingly, few examples in England's essays of individuals who found it necessary to give up their affiliation with the group rather than submit to orders they could not follow in good conscience. The conclusion of England's essay on the paradox of selfhood, however, hints at how the paradox is suspended, rather than resolved, in his reading of these historical examples. He returns to a favorite quotation from Michael Novak, a conservative Catholic thinker, who expanded on Martin Luther's dictum that "marriage is the school of love." England quoted the following paragraphs of Novak's exegesis on many occasions:

> Marriage is an assault upon the lonely, atomic ego. Marriage is a threat to the solitary individual. Marriage does impose grueling, humbling, baffling, and frustrating responsibilities. Yet if one supposes that precisely such things are the preconditions for all true liberation, marriage is not the enemy of moral development in adults. Quite the opposite . . .
>
> . . . My bonds to [my wife and children] hold me back (and my wife even more) from many sorts of opportunities. And yet these do not feel like bonds. They are, I know, my liberation. They force me to be a different sort of human being, in a way in which I want and need to be forced.[21]

Sometimes, as at the end of the essay on selfhood and integrity, England's invocation of Novak seems like an evasion of the problem. Several of England's essays move from discussion of life as a member of a conservative church—an institution that would seem to demand that the paradox of integrity and obedience always be resolved in favor of obedience—to apparently unrelated discussions of marriage and family life. But for England, these things *are* related—the paradox of individual integrity and the requirements of a committed, loving relationship is most clearly illustrated by the covenant of marriage. A covenant, in England's view, is "a free, conscientious binding of the individual will to God, to an eternal partner, to a community."[22] And it is only in such a covenant that the individual can maintain both integrity and loyalty. Thus, for instance, B. H. Roberts maintained integrity long enough to articulate his decision not as a capitulation to Joseph F. Smith, but as a choice to continue in the work of the institution he loved and freely chose. Levi Savage maintained his integrity by publicly and repeatedly insisting that his leaders' claim of revelation should not be privileged over what could be known by reason, and by choosing to go with the handcart company as a deliberate act of love rather than blind obedience. Orson Pratt's final submission to Brigham Young's doctrinal authority was not, as his first retractions of his teachings had been, coerced, but was freely chosen and voluntarily offered. John D. Lee's choice *not* to honor his own conscience, but instead to doubt his own witness of God's will and obey the voice of the mob looks at first exactly like the decisions of Pratt and Roberts to submit to the decrees of church authorities. Importantly, though, Lee's decision is not made *in relationship*—both Roberts and Pratt wrestled with their consciences in private agony, but, importantly, they also met repeatedly with those they felt were demanding irrational submission from them and did not yield until they were able to act out of love rather than mere obedience.

England's answering abstract questions about integrity and authority by reference to the concrete challenges of marriage points toward another paradox England limns, though rarely explicitly: the relationship between the holy and the ordinary. Theologically, Mormonism gives warrant for collapsing the distance between the two, in the Doctrine and Covenants' proposition that "all spirit is matter" (Doctrine and Covenants 131:7), but discovering how to live in a modern world they believe to be enchanted has always challenged the Saints. England sometimes seems to come down heavily on the side of practical reason, as in the case of Levi Savage, in which he praises Savage's advocacy of well-informed caution over the recklessness of Franklin Richards's claim to revelatory absolutism. On the other hand, England wrote (and published!) an essay about the times (plural!) he laid his hands on the family car to give it a blessing, and it was "healed" to facilitate his church service or get his family safely home. In that essay, "Blessing the Chevrolet," England lays out the questions incited by his faith:

> How about our free agency and our need to learn to solve our own problems and be maturely independent—not like infants always asking for help? How fit all this with the Lord's assurances that he makes his sun and rain to come down equally on all his children—the just and the unjust? How about all that suffering, apparently uninterrupted by God,

in the Sub-Sahara famine, Southeast Asia's constant bloodshed, deserted children in South American cities, the emotional destruction during slow death in American nursing homes? Couldn't God have veered the typhoon that killed thousands in Bangladesh or the earthquake that killed thousands in Iran, as well as guide the mechanic to straighten out the timing on my Chev or me to someone who could cure my car?[23]

The essay ends with a shrug, England resigned to live with the mystery and to continue offering up the stuff of his daily life to be consecrated. Here, as elsewhere, England's characteristic response to the irresolvable tensions he articulates is action, and particularly religious practice. The argument England never quite makes explicitly is that religious practice integrates unanswerable questions into a life of meaningful action—of trying, essaying, proving contraries. Paradoxes that resist rational resolutions can nevertheless be meaningfully lived.

Atonement

England's insistence that paradox should not be resolved, but transcended, leads him to a distinctive view of atonement. Like the concepts of paradox and dialogue, the idea of atonement is central to England's thought, a persistent theme. His first extensive published treatment of the topic was in a sermon delivered to Stanford students in 1966, which was published in *Dialogue* later that year, titled, "That They Might Not Suffer: The Gift of the Atonement." Near the end of his BYU career, he said, "I teach the Atonement in every class because I find it explored in all great literature."[24] The term and the concept of atonement come up frequently in essays on other topics, because England's privileging of dialogue and paradox generally requires some sort of reconciliation to hold together disparate ideas, arguments, or interlocutors. Besides that first essay, his major interventions on the theme include the essay "Easter Sunday" (1986) and his final, posthumously published essay, "The Weeping God of Mormonism."

In "That They Might Not Suffer," England describes the consequences of the Fall as a threefold alienation:

> We find ourselves cut off from *others*, relating to each other as things, not as personal images of the eternal God; unable to say our truest thoughts and feelings to each other. . . .

We find ourselves cut off from *God*, without a deep sense of joyful relation to him; witnessing him die in us and our civilization through the dead forms of our concepts of him and the inflexible forms of our response to him in the world. . . .

And we find ourselves cut off from *ourselves*. We sin. We act contrary to our image of ourselves and break our deepest integrity. . . . We . . . find the self of action tragically divided against the self of belief.[25]

As the antidote to all of these forms of alienation, England offers "atonement," a word whose etymology he unpacks as simply "at-one-ment," the process of making separate things into a unified whole.

England's emphasis on personal alienation that requires reconciliation is unusual in Mormon discourse about sin. More often, Mormons speak of sinful actions that are offensive to God, and the need to have these actions "blotted out" before returning to live with God. Satisfaction and penal substitution theories underlie many Mormon descriptions of the mechanism of atonement. England's description seems more closely aligned with Abelard's moral influence theory—Abelard posits that Christ's death effectuates atonement not by satisfying a debt or paying a ransom, but by inspiring human beings to love God and change from their sinful ways. Later, England became interested in the scapegoat theory of French philosopher René Girard. Girard suggested that one reason people are able to accept the idea of Christ as suffering vicariously for sin is that human beings are inclined to diffuse conflict by attaching guilt to an innocent third party, a scapegoat.

England consistently prioritizes the individual psychological experience of reconciliation, first with the self and then with God. England accepts the Mormon notion of a *felix culpa*—fortunate Fall, in which exile from the Garden of Eden was a brave and necessary step in God's plan for human salvation. In England's gloss of this Mormon doctrine, atonement is not necessary to overcome human beings' estrangement from God through original sin, a corrupted nature that God cannot abide. Instead, England locates the barrier to human reconciliation with God not in God's demand for righteousness, but in human beings' own sense of justice:

Atonement is necessary to help human beings be "at one" with their own highest ideals—the inevitable alienation of the self when we discover that "that which I would do, I do not, and that which I would not, I do" is overcome by the fact that Christ extends love to us when we ourselves recognize that we have violated our own moral convictions. The fact that Christ fulfilled all moral ideals and is a worthy judge, is what makes his love efficacious in overcoming our own self-condemnation.[26]

Because God's love is here offered unconditionally by a perfect being, whom human beings can recognize as a righteous judge, it has power to free them from guilt. England uses "guilt" to describe not culpability for wrong action, but the emotional experience of guilt, which prevents human beings from wanting to be with God.

England also suggests a different ordering of the process of repentance. Rather than atonement as the end result of a process of human contrition and reformation, he suggests that atonement is a necessary catalyst. This idea apparently germinated in a class with Lowell Bennion, in which they discussed a passage from Alma 34, in which the death of Jesus is called "an infinite and eternal sacrifice," which transcends the human sense of justice:

> Now there is not any man that can sacrifice his own blood which will atone for the sins of another. Now, if a man murdereth, behold will our law, which is just, take the life of his brother? I say unto you, Nay.
>
> But the law requireth the life of him who hath murdered; therefore there can be nothing which is short of an infinite atonement which will suffice for the sins of the world.
>
> Therefore, it is expedient that there should be a great and last sacrifice, and then shall there be, or it is expedient there should be, a stop to the shedding of blood. . . .
>
> . . . This being the intent of this last sacrifice, to bring about the bowels of mercy, which overpowereth justice, and bringeth about means unto men that they may have faith unto repentance.
>
> And thus mercy can satisfy the demands of justice, and encircles them in the arms of safety, while he that exercises no faith unto repentance is exposed to the whole law of the demands of justice.

England's reading of this passage notes the human resistance to anything like penal substitution. "The demands of justice that Amulek is talking about, which must be overpowered, are from *man's own sense of justice*." Human beings' own moral reasoning apparatus as well as their understanding of what makes laws just make it difficult to accept the notion that Christ's death could mitigate human guilt. Thus, England argues, atonement with God—the acceptance of Christ's unconditional love—is a necessary catalyst for the process of repentance, which allows forgiveness and reconciliation that overcome alienation from the self and other human beings.[27]

England asserts that atonement is not a necessary corrective to Adam's actions in Eden, amplifying the tenet from the Mormon Articles of Faith that "We believe men will be punished for their own sins, and not for Adam's transgression."[28] In fact, England argues, Mormon readings of the Creation narrative interpret Adam's actions as part of God's plan from the beginning, a necessary step towards moral agency: "Mormons see [Adam] as a great, courageous figure who chose a difficult path necessary to his and all men's progression—the way of estrangement and reconciliation, of sin and resultant openness to redeeming love."[29]

England conceives of atonement as related primarily to repairing the alienation between an individual and himself, and the individual and God. He explicitly rejects theories that posit that the atonement works outside of the individual's perception on the universe or on God: "The redemptive effect of the Atonement depends on how an *individual* responds to it, rather than some independent effect on the universe or God, which theories such as the ransom theory, the substitution theory, the satisfaction theory, etc. all seem to imply."[30] He mentions Paul Tillich as his source for the idea that "the most difficult thing for us to do is to accept our acceptance."

More than twenty years after this first published essay on atonement, England was still working out its mechanism and psychology. In the impressionistic essay "Easter Weekend," England tries, through the conceit of an apostrophe directed to Jesus himself, to find a description:

> It hurts very much to think of you. How could you suffer not only our pains but our sicknesses and infirmities? . . . Everyone says you didn't sin, that you were always perfect. But how then could you learn how to help us?
>
> Could it be that your very willingness to know the actual pain and confusion and despair of sin, to join with us fully, is what saves us? It's true, I feel your condescension in that; I feel you coming down from your formidable, separate height as my Judge and Conscience. I feel you next to me as my friend. . . . So how can I refuse to accept myself, refuse to be whole again, if you, though my Judge whom I hide from, know exactly what I feel and still accept me?[31]

The theme of atonement also occupies the final essay England wrote, which was published posthumously in 2002. "The Weeping God of Mormonism" connects England's attempts at a personal understanding of atonement with the larger questions about the nature of God that animated his exchange with Bruce McConkie and some of the conflict at BYU in the late 1980s and 1990s. The essay directly challenges the neo-orthodox emphasis on human inferiority to and distance from God that had been ascendant in the writings of some BYU Religious Education professors, and increasingly popular among General Authorities of the church, beginning with the writings of J. Reuben Clark. England traces the history of both strains of thought in Mormonism, and presciently describes the social and political positions that might follow from differing theologies.

England particularly singles out BYU professor of ancient scripture Stephen Robinson as an exemplar of the kind of theology he believes is a danger to traditional Mormon conceptions of God. Robinson, who became well known among Mormons after publishing a book called *Believing Christ* in 1992, grounds his discussion of atonement and grace in a Book of Mormon passage in 2 Nephi (25:23), which asserts that "we know it is by grace that we are saved, after all we can do." The phrase "after all we can do" functions as an elastic clause allowing a view of salvation that is mostly works-based, but lets grace into the gaps in human capacity, as in the book's "Parable of the Bicycle." In this "parable," Robinson describes a time when his seven-year-old daughter wanted a bicycle. He told her that if she saved all her pennies, she could buy one. She dutifully saved for some time, then came to him one day and asked for a bike. When they went to the store, she saw the price tags on bicycles and began to cry that she would never have enough. He made a deal with her that if she would give him all she had—$0.61—he would pay the rest. Robinson analogizes that fatherly action to Jesus' atonement.

> We all desperately want the celestial kingdom. We want to be with our Father in Heaven. But no matter how hard we try, we come up short. At some point all of us must realize, "I can't do this by myself. I need help." Then it is that the Savior says, in effect, All right, you're not perfect. But what *can* you do? Give me all you have, and I'll do the rest.
>
> He still requires our best effort. We must keep trying. But the good news is that having done all we can, it is enough. We may not be person-

ally perfect yet, but because of our covenant with the Savior, we can rely on *his* perfection, and his perfection will get us through.[32]

England's fiercest disagreement with Robinson, however, is not about this theory of atonement, but about Robinson's 1997 book *How Wide the Divide: A Mormon and an Evangelical in Conversation*, coauthored with Evangelical theologian Craig L. Blomberg. England takes issue particularly with a passage in which Robinson declares that the notion of a "finite, limited, or changeable god" is "repugnant" to Mormons. While Robinson's is a strong formulation of the argument for a Mormon god who is omnipotent, omniscient, and infinite, he was certainly not making a radical departure from the teachings of his contemporaries. Besides Bruce R. McConkie's prolific and influential writings and speeches on the topic, other apostles including Mark E. Peterson, Ezra Taft Benson, and Boyd K. Packer, had used similar language for decades.[33] In *Mormon Neo-Orthodoxy: A Crisis Theology*, O. Kendall White identified BYU religion professors as early as 1960 beginning to lament that Mormons did not sufficiently appreciate God's uniqueness, otherness, and glory.[34] BYU religion professors Hyrum Andrus, David Yarn, Glenn Pearson, and others deemphasized earlier Mormon teachings, like those of Roberts and Widtsoe, that stressed the value of human reason and human learning. Instead, these writers insisted on the differences between human beings and God, and the inadequacy of human knowledge. In 1961, Pearson wrote that "God is infinite. Men are finite. God is not the servant of law but the master of it." Even scriptural passages that had often been used to encourage learning and study, like "the glory of God is intelligence," were reframed as having nothing to do with human or "secular" knowledge, but instead being knowledge of the salvific principles of the Christian gospel. White traces this skeptical view of "worldly" knowledge to Clark, who said, as early as 1938, that the primary duty of teachers throughout the Church Education System, including BYU, was "to teach the gospel": "You do have an interest in matters purely cultural and in matters of purely secular knowledge, but, I repeat again for emphasis, your chief interest, your essential and all but sole duty, is to teach the gospel of the Lord Jesus Christ as that has been revealed in these latter days."[35] In Robinson's work, and in that of his colleague Robert Millett, who worked with him to sponsor interfaith dialogues with Evangelical Christians, this emphasis on the differences between humans and God and the inadequacy of human reason

made room for a greater acceptance of the role of grace in human salvation. "Traditional" Mormon doctrine—articulated by Widtsoe, Talmage,
and Roberts—did not deny the necessity of grace, but emphasized human
perfectibility and gave more weight to human beings' own contribution to
their salvation. An astute observer of Mormon culture, Douglas Davies,
suggests two reasons for the appeal of grace to Mormon thinkers in the
1980s and 1990s—one pastoral, and one ecclesiological. Davies writes that
the heightened emphasis on grace "answers the needs of devoted Saints,
laboring under apparently impossible goals of achievement." The possibility of drawing on this strain of Christian discourse, Davies surmises, may
be due in part to Mormonism's maturing confidence of its stature among
Christian churches.[36]

England certainly had intuited that pastoral need—the felt longing for
acceptance from God, despite one's imperfections, is the central focus of
his theory of atonement. England, however, does not recognize the possibility that the neo-orthodox version of Mormonism might be answering
a need in Mormon culture. In response to Robinson's denial that Mormons
believe in a god who is finite or changeable, England recapitulates some of
the sources that he had enumerated in "Perfection and Progression: Two
Ways to Talk About God" to argue for God's finitude and the possibility
of God's progression. He then turns to the ethical problems that result
from believing in an omniscient and omnipotent god. He poses a rather
petulant version of the problem of evil (which he admits is "somewhat of
a caricature"):

> If [God] was already perfect, why did he "need" to create this mess at
> all, and if he's all-powerful, why couldn't he just make an Adam and Eve
> who would have done things right in the first place, or (since they were
> made out of nothing) destroy them and start over, again and again until
> he got the world he wanted, or at least just send those sinners who fail
> his plan back into nothingness rather than to eternal torment (or make
> Christian teaching available to more than ten percent of his children, or
> prevent the holocaust, etc., etc.)?[37]

To counter such a God and such a world, England extols the ethical appeal
of a God "who exists with other eternal beings whom it is his work and glory
to help develop in the ways he himself has developed, so they can enjoy his
work and glory, too." England takes his description of this God from the

account of the prophet Enoch, from the book of Moses in the Pearl of Great Price. In this story, Enoch has a vision of God, who is surveying the Earth, and is dismayed by the wickedness of the people he has created. When God begins to weep, Enoch raises the paradox of God's omnipotence and the world in which human beings suffer, asking God why he weeps—"how it is thou canst weep, seeing thou art holy, and from all eternity to all eternity?" Weeping, as England points out, is a typical human response to events or circumstances a person cannot control or master. Enoch seems to expect that a God who is benevolent and stands outside of human boundaries of time and space should respond differently than a mortal who has less power to change the course of eternity. God's response is to point Enoch to look at his "brethren," his fellow human beings who are choosing to do evil. He points out the difference between what God has commanded—that they should love one another—and what they are choosing—to "hate their own blood." In this difference—the difference between divine command and human choice—England locates the foundational theological principal of "agency"—human freedom of the will. And in God's tears, England locates the abrogation of divine omnipotence—this God *cannot* override human agency, because human agency, and the real evil that comes of it, is foundational to the universe in which this God exists and creates: "The theodicy revealed to Enoch and foundational to Mormonism's orthodoxy denies the other pole of the paradox: God's omnipotence. God allows evil because there is much of it he can't prevent or do away with. Therefore, like a human, he weeps."[38]

England posits that God can interfere with evil, but cannot eliminate it entirely, because to do so would violate the laws of a universe which existed, along with human intelligences, before God became God. The "intractable nature" of this universe demands that human freedom should have "maximum latitude" to make meaningful choices in learning to grapple with natural law.

England contrasts this view with the sorts of theodicies that rely on the implication, from the book of Job, that if human beings could see their suffering from the vantage point of God, from the time "when the morning starts sang together," their perception of evil would change. Enoch's weeping God suggests that God's perception of evil is similar to human beings' experience of it, and that he mourns as they do. "I believe God means we, like Job, must recognize that the universe itself, not a finite God, is the 'proprietor' of those things; we *could not* have all the good of it, including the means to grow and know beauty and have joy and become more God-like, without the evil, not because God is that way, but because the universe, which he did not make, is that way."[39] England takes scriptural warrant for this view partly from the Book of Mormon—from the passages in 2 Nephi cited above, and from another verse in Alma which insists that without allowing the opposition in all things that makes meaningful choice possible, with both the suffering and joy that flow from that human freedom, that "God would cease to be God."

On the other hand, England acknowledges that Joseph Smith and other Latter-day Saints have interpreted other verses from the Book of Mormon to denote a God who "has all power" quite literally, in the tradition of definitions of omnipotence from other Christian denominations. He admits, crucially, that the "attractions of a weeping God may be mostly a matter of basic temperament rather than overwhelming rational evidence or even authority." Temperament, though, seems not to be morally neutral in England's view: "Some of us in each age seem genuinely attracted to the securities of an absolute, sovereign, justice-oriented God and some to the adventuresomeness of an open, progressive universe and a limited but infinitely loving God working with us eternal mortal agents." England suggests that people with an "absolutistic temperament" tend to be less tolerant and less willing to coexist with those whose views differ. Although he says that believing in a weeping, compassionate God rather than a punitive one does not "necessarily" make people more compassionate, he suggests that the believer who "imagines Christ's suffering as a necessary and sufficient substitute for our sins, demanded by God's justice and available to those whom he chooses to save into eternal bliss while the rest burn in hell," may create for themselves an ethical "escape clause," where the promise of future justice excuses them from striving to create more justice in the present.[40]

England's urgency in this essay is palpable, as is his sense of personal involvement. He reads the cultural and political divides between the Saints as a consequence of differing fundamental theological commitments. He cites playwright David Hare, "who believes, after careful observation, that such a belief tends ultimately to limit the quality and persistence of Christian service, that justice on this earth matters less if justice will one day be delivered by another." While he acknowledges the impossibility of proving that Mormons with the "absolutistic temperament" and belief in a God who is distant and inscrutable to human beings are less concerned about justice, he nevertheless concludes that "those who can believe in the weeping God of Mormonism . . . must stand with . . . the compassionate, passionate agnostics of the world in making it better, confident that God is doing and will do all he can, but that what we do and don't do has irrevocable, sometimes tragic, consequences." He describes neo-orthodoxy as an "assault," even as he says that better theology is needed "to stem our inclinations to various forms of violence with each other."[41]

The tone of this essay is uncharacteristic of England—editing might have softened its rhetorical edges if he had lived longer. But in its raw urgency, it connects the themes of much of England's work. His commitment to the progressive and progressing God he read in the sermons of Joseph Smith and Brigham Young, and in the work of B. H. Roberts and other early twentieth-century leaders, informed his lifelong dedication to learning and teaching, his political activism, and his complicated efforts to consecrate his intellect to the church he loved. England carefully studied the nineteenth- and early twentieth-century struggle over which theology would predominate, and he was a significant participant in the late twentieth-century recapitulation of that struggle, in his conflict with Bruce R. McConkie. There was reason for him to fear that his exile from BYU had left neo-orthodoxy in the ascendancy for the moment, at least within the Church Educational System. In the decades following his death, however, the picture seems like one England would have found more hopeful. Theologians like Adam Miller and Terryl and Fiona Givens are attracted to the same strains of older Mormon thought that animated England's thought, and their works have a wide audience among a certain swath of English-speaking Latter-day Saints, particularly those involved in academic Mormon studies. Miller's work was recently quoted by an apostle, Todd Christofferson, in a BYU devotional address, suggesting that at least one current apostle does not entirely share McConkie's notion that professors ought to echo apostles or remain silent.

One of the Givenses' popular books is titled *The God Who Weeps*—a title clearly reminiscent of England's "The Weeping God of Mormonism." They read in the Creation story of Genesis a relationship between God and humankind that entails a particular sort of relation; by eating the fruit of the Tree of Knowledge, Adam and Eve become subject to death, and capable of sin. But the Givenses suggest that Mormon doctrine makes the capacity for sin a mechanism by which the distance between God and humanity is lessened, rather than increased. Adam and Eve can sin precisely because they have come to see the same moral distinctions as God does. "Humankind and God," they write, "now share a common moral awareness, a common capacity to judge between right and wrong, a common capacity for love." The capacity for moral judgment, the agency to make moral choices, and the capacity for love affirm that humans are capable of learning and growing to become *like* God, affirming their essential kinship.[42]

In this volume, the Givenses do not directly address the question of whether God progresses, nor do they dwell on God's omniscience or omnipotence in relationship to human beings. Nevertheless, their emphasis throughout the book on human beings' kinship and likeness with the divine runs counter to the neo-orthodox emphasis on God's majesty and distance from humankind. The God Who Weeps seems very much like England's "being who exists with other eternal beings whom it is his work and glory to help develop in the ways he himself has developed, so they can enjoy his work and glory, too."[43]

In *Wrestling the Angel*, Terryl Givens summarizes the situation of Mormon theology related to God's finitude and progression: "The simple truth is, Mormons are divided on more than the question of language. That God has a body of finite dimensions; occupies space, rejoices and weeps; and adds continually to his posterity and creations, while bringing about human salvation subject to the constraints of moral agency, elicits no disagreement. Whether these conditions add up to a finite, limited God who is 'progressing' is still a subject of debate."[44]

The work of Terryl and Fiona Givens has attracted interest among "mainstream" Mormons as well as academics. Their books are sold at church-owned Deseret Book, with a network of bookstores and substantial online distribution. Because it is so closely affiliated with the official church. The acceptance and popularity of the Givenses' work suggests that perhaps Eugene England's theological writing was in some sense conservative—by teaching and championing this older strain of Mormon thought, England preserved it for a moment when it was again well-suited for its time.

It remains to be seen whether a church that is making a transition from decades of rapid growth that depended heavily on centralized authority to being a truly worldwide church might return to some of the theological expansiveness of its roots.

The current situation, as illustrated by the success of the Givenses' and Adam Miller's work, suggests a movement away from the cyclical liberalization and retrenchment that one can discern in the mid-twentieth-century doctrinal development of Mormonism—the pull from intellectuals like England (or, before him, Witdsoe and Roberts) and the authoritative pushback from church leaders like Joseph F. Smith and Bruce R. McConkie. The growth of the church, the bureaucratic demands on its governing quorums, and the apparent disinclination of apostles after McConkie to produce systematizing theological treatises seem to have returned the church to something more like its early doctrinal tolerance. Both Mormon thinkers and astute non-Mormon observers, from anthropologist Mark Leone in the 1970s to philosopher Stephen Webb in the 2010s, have identified theological "flexibility" and "informality" as characteristic of the faith, whether they regard it as a particular strength or a peculiar weakness. It may be that Eugene England was simply unfortunate to have lived in a singular moment in the development of Mormonism when anxiety about doctrinal coherence was at its apex. The late 1970s through the early 1990s are beginning to seem, in retrospect, like a moment of unusual tension between Mormon intellectual factions. That tension seems to have dissipated more than it has been resolved, so it is possible that these questions will again lead to conflict, but there are good reasons to hope they will not.

The urgency of England's theological concern in his final essay leads him to a more polemical tone than most of his work, and this is its real pathos. In the deepest sort of irony, Eugene England's formula for living with unsolvable philosophical problems turns out to be the necessary and only possible resolution of the theological conflict that so distressed him at the end of his life—your neighbor's wrongheaded views about eternal progression aren't relevant when he needs help with yardwork; your own mistaken scriptural interpretation won't spoil the taste of the casserole your neighbor brings when you are sick. What England saw clearly, almost all of the time, was that Mormonism's genius lies in refusing to conflate faithfulness and orthodoxy. England's life, despite the conflict with authority that blighted the end of his career, is a testament to the liberal possibilities of Mormon theology and the difficult, hopeful path of remaining faithful to those ideas while making a home in an institutional church with shifting orthodoxies. As his birth coincided with the death of important Mormon thinkers who saw Mormonism's liberal possibilities, Eugene England's death coincided with the emergence of a new generation of Mormon scholars who are finding new ways to resist or simply ignore the neo-orthodox currents that thwarted England and obscured the work of the last generation's liberal thinkers. Though they may no longer inhabit the safe valleys where England worked out his understanding of Mormonism, these intellectuals' horizons also stretch beyond old demarcations of conservative and liberal, and their vision is not directed exclusively at a hierarchical American institution. These scholars, Mormon and non-Mormon alike, inherit not only England's thought, but the lessons of his life, particularly his appreciation for the kind of lived religion that always escapes efforts at correlation, and to which orthodoxy and heterodoxy are irrelevant. England's greatest legacy will be his example of thinking differently than his fellow Saints and loving them just the same.

Bibliographic Essay

The major principles I have outlined in this brief introduction to Eugene England's thought seem to me to be the fundamental organizing themes, the hermeneutic toolkit of his work. I have barely hinted, however, at the number and range of texts and sources in which England worked out those interpretive themes. The following brief topical bibliography sketches more of England's work and will, I hope, provide interested readers with a roadmap for entering the rich and varied landscape of England's creative intellectual and spiritual legacy.

Readers interested in Eugene England can start at the website organized by the England Family Foundation at eugeneengland.org. The site houses biographical information, reminiscences from friends and family members, and several of the most essential personal essays, as well as a few of his published academic articles. A bibliography page there provides helpful links to more of his books and essays, and gives a sense of the breadth of his interests. Other online resources include Signature Books' excellent online library (http://signaturebookslibrary.org/), which hosts *Dialogues with Myself*, *Bright Angels and Familiars*, *Making Peace*, and *Tending the Garden*.

Pedagogy, Teaching, Values

As an undergraduate at the University of Utah, England took several classes at the LDS Institute taught by Lowell Bennion. England was excited by the content of those classes as well as attentive to Bennion's methods. In a remembrance, he noted that Bennion was "a better teacher than writer" (though he was a fine writer). England describes Bennion's class presentations as focused on a "single, fundamental, clear idea" and involving many more questions than answers. Bennion taught religion not as "a dogmatic set of answers," but as "a unified set of tools, principles, ideas, and feelings that can provide a permanent, growing basis for dealing with the bewildering variety of questions and challenges that life poses." England also admired Bennion's clearly articulated principles of epistemology—that principles must be consistent in their entire context (including especially the repeated fundamental teachings of the scriptures) and can be verified by experience, authority, and spiritual witness.[1]

England attended graduate school as a Danforth Fellow, and was influenced by the Danforth Foundation's longstanding commitment to developing academics who would be thoughtful teachers as well as talented researchers. At Stanford, and then at St. Olaf College, Brigham Young University, and Utah Valley State College, England focused on developing programs that would treat students as whole human beings, not narrow specialists just training to earn money in a particular discipline. Along with encouraging students to understand calculus as a feat of human *imagination* equal to Shakespeare, the Honors Program he helped shape at BYU included adventures like

> a four day "Wilderness Trek," where they had to confront such fundamental physical challenges as hiking twenty miles on no food, together butchering and consuming an entire sheep, . . . handling snakes and rappelling down hundred foot cliffs, all this after having read Thoreau's *Walden*, and followed up by the responsibility to write their own "Walden," their own extended synthesis of their experience and its relevance to more serious and more usual challenges than those posed by a mere snake or living alone by a pond.[2]

England was a champion of religious colleges generally, not just Mormon ones, and recommended religious colleges to young Mormons who could not attend BYU. He valued the freedom to discuss religious and spiritual ideas in their academic contexts and connect ideas from across the full range of human endeavor. His final public presentation at Utah Valley State College (now Utah Valley University) before his death expressed his hope for this kind of learning. He defined academic freedom as the "free exploration and expression which Mormon theology itself claims is necessary for individual salvation" and cites a favorite passage from LDS Apostle Hugh B. Brown as "the official Mormon position on academic freedom":[3]

One of the most important things in the world is freedom of the mind; from this all other freedoms spring. Such freedom is necessarily dangerous, for one cannot think right without running the risk of thinking wrong, but generally more thinking is the antidote for the evils that spring from wrong thinking. . . . Think through every proposition that is submitted to you and be unafraid to express your opinions, with proper respect for those to whom you talk and proper acknowledgement of your own shortcomings.

A colleague at BYU recalled England's focus on educational method, as well as his quirky enthusiasms:

He was especially keen on *Sir Gawain and the Green Knight*. It had been a paper that he had built in his undergraduate or graduate years, and it was based on the ideas of Johan Huizinga, the great Dutch philosopher: the idea that we are organized after the pattern of games, in our religions, in our societies, and so forth. He would show that pattern . . ., and he would show the game being played out in Sir Gawain's life. He would get so caught up in helping [students] see and become conscious of their role as a pawn in the game scheme. . . .

It was all inter-related with this idea of game and can you find the patterns in the world in different disciplines, and how can we understand those patterns well enough that we can become not determined by those patterns, but agents to live within those patterns and move around in them in more fruitful ways.[4]

His students' recollections are in some ways a better index to his teaching methods than his own writings and some of their tributes are linked below. However, England's own thinking on pedagogy is an intriguing engagement with questions about higher education that were being asked in the late twentieth century, many of which can profitably be asked perennially.

England, Eugene. "Becoming Brigham Young's University." In *On the Lord's Errand: The Purposes and Possibilities of Brigham Young University*. Provo, UT: Brigham Young University, 1985.
———. "Brigham Young's University and the Music of Hope." *BYU Today* 37.5 (October 1983): 17–19.
———. "Knowledge without Zeal." A statement on honors education at BYU given to the Humanities College faculty, 7 Dec. 1978. eugeneengland.org/wp-content/uploads/sbi/articles/1978_sc_op_004.pdf.

———. "The Quest for Authentic Faculty Power." *Soundings: An Interdisciplinary Journal* 52.2 (1969): 196–217.

———. Response to "Towards a New Humanism," by Ronald Lee. In *A Teacher's Faith and Values*, edited by Eugene England and Erling Jorstad, 134–41. Northfield, MN: St. Olaf College, 1973.

England, Eugene, and Erling Jorstad, eds. *A Teacher's Faith and Values*. Northfield, MN: St. Olaf College, 1973.

Monson, Diane Saderup. "Eugene England—Master Teacher: The BYU Years." *Sunstone* 121 (Jan. 2002): 25–30.

Pingree, Allison. "A Dining Room Table." *Dialogue: A Journal of Mormon Thought* 35.1 (Spring 2002): 23–26.

Feminism, Gender

England was an observer of the second wave of feminism in the United States, and the ripples it made among Mormon women. He encouraged women to write, and then edited, anthologized, published, and championed their work. Much of England's own writing on women exalts them in essentialist terms, as natural healers and peacemakers, exempt from the cycles of revenge and violence that provide so much of the drama in Shakespeare and the scriptures.

England draws on historical Mormon theology about the Fall to criticize contemporary Mormon discourse and practice. "Are All Alike unto God?" summarizes his most frequent arguments against sexism: "I believe that God, as part of the Restoration, gave revelations and inspired direction to Joseph Smith that directly countered in remarkable ways the prevailing racism and sexism of Western culture. in doctrine, and even in practice for awhile, the Church was relatively free from those evils."

Polygamy, he argues, required the reintroduction of some sexist theologies about the Fall, and current practices, which limit women's participation in church governance and forbid their ordination to the priesthood, may be based in such mistaken popular theologies. This argument is contradicted, however, by primary evidence from Mormon polygamous wives who wrote in their diaries and other personal writings, as well as in the *Woman's Exponent* (a nineteenth- and early twentieth-century women's newspaper published in Utah, which advocated women's suffrage and equal treatment under the law and in business and society). They understood and embraced the notion of the fortunate Fall, with Eve leading the way toward progress *at the same time as* they defended the practice of polygamy.

When England turned from abstract and theological considerations of the place of women to describing the actual plight of contemporary Mormon women, he sometimes stumbled. His "We Need to Liberate Mormon Men," for instance, sounds patronizing or willfully ignorant of the legitimate complaints of Mormon women about their place in the church and in Mormon culture:

> In the past twenty years an increasing number of voices . . . have claimed that the rights and freedoms of women have been severely restricted under various patriarchal systems, particularly religious ones—and that women have thus been suppressed, prevented from their possible development and expression as creative, free human beings. Mormonism, with its strongly authoritarian male priesthood and family centered theology, has been attacked as an extreme example of this suppression by religious patriarchy.
>
> . . . I have found nothing to support these claims in my own experience with Mormon women, especially Charlotte England. However, many bright and good people feel *something* is wrong, so I began to look for evidence one way or the other in my own field of scholarship, Mormon literature.
>
> The evidence, I am convinced, shows that Mormon women are more free, more daring, inventive, original in thought and unique in voice than Mormon men. In quantity and quality of literary production, certainly one of the great measures of freedom and creativity, they are more liberated than men under the "patriarchy."[5]

Despite occasional awkwardness, England's championing of women's voices was effective. He was a lifelong advocate of women's writing and women's speaking out. One of his first major efforts to encourage women's writing was the "Pink Issue" of *Dialogue*. Claudia Bushman and a group of Mormon feminists in Boston approached him about the possibility of contributing, and he turned over the editing of an entire issue to them. It was a landmark publication—one of a few issues of *Dialogue* that have become collector's items—and it helped launch that group of women (and others) into publishing Mormon women's voices in *Exponent II*. In one especially lovely tribute to England after his death, Mormon novelist and filmmaker Margaret Blair Young recalled, "Gene became one of the primary forces in my finally telling the hard stories my heart knew so well," a sentiment echoed by many of his students and other women he inspired by his sincere praise and candid critiques of their work.[6] He sought out and published women's work in *Dialogue* and encouraged women's leadership in the Mormon History Association, Association for Mormon Letters, *Sunstone*, and other organizations in which he participated and had influence. He was a feminist ally *avant la lettre*.

England, Eugene. "Are All Alike unto God?: Prejudice against Blacks and Women in Popular Mormon Thought." *Sunstone* 15.2 (Mar./Apr. 1990): 21–31.

———. "Are Women More Free under the Patriarchy?: The Evidence of Mormon Literature." *Mormon Letters Annual 1983* (1984): 131–50.

———. "Healing and Making Peace—In the World and the Church," *Sunstone* 15.6 (Dec. 1991): 36–46.

———. "How Mormon Women Figure Things Out." Review of Mary Lythgoe Bradford's *Mormon Women Speak: A Collection of Essays. Sunstone* 3.4/5 (Apr./May 1983): 29–31.

———. "A New Era for Mormon Women and Men." In *Women of Wisdom and Knowledge: Talks Selected from the BYU Women's Conference, 1989,* edited by Marie Cornwall and Susan Howe, 136–43. Salt Lake City, UT: Deseret Book, 1990.

———. "On Being Male and Melchizedek." *Dialogue: A Journal of Mormon Thought* 23.4 (Winter 1990): 64–79.

———. "We Need to Liberate Mormon Men: The Evidence of Mormon Literature." *Exponent II* 9.3 (Spring 1983): 4–5.

Mormon Literature

England believed both that Mormon literature was great and that it had not achieved the full stature that a literature drawing on the religious depths of Mormonism could aspire to. Although he especially loved and championed the personal essay, there is no aspect of Mormon literature that did not benefit from his engagement. He wrote dozens and dozens of reviews, profiles of Mormon authors, and bibliographic guides, as well as editing or coediting three volumes of historic and contemporary Mormon literature. The proportion of his work dedicated to championing other authors is remarkable.

He edited and coedited anthologies of Mormon poetry, short stories, and critical essays. His introductions to those volumes are excellent and succinct histories of Mormon efforts in each genre. He also worked for many years on a bibliographic essay (published in 1995, then revised and published again after his death), titled "Mormon Literature: Progress and Prospects," which is a helpful guide both to the best of Mormon literature and to the issues he believed Mormon writers would have to grapple with and transcend to achieve the greatness predicted and hoped for by Mormon prophets. He describes one pole of the debate about what this greatness would be like as aligned with the view of church leaders like Apostle Boyd K. Packer and BYU English professor Richard Cracroft that too much contemporary Mormon literature is flawed—"too imitative of flawed contemporary critical and moral trends and thus untrue to Mormon traditions and values." Packer urged distinctiveness based on religious content: "Our worship and devotion will remain as unique from the world as the Church is different from the world." England locates the other pole of the debate as the vision articulated by church president Spencer W. Kimball, who encouraged a wider range of expression and content:

> For years I have been waiting for someone to do justice in recording in song and story and painting and sculpture the story of the restoration, the reestablishment of the kingdom of God on earth, the struggles and frustrations; the apostasies and inner revolutions and counter-revolutions of those first decades; of the exodus; of the counter-reactions; of the transitions; of the persecution days; of the miracle man, Joseph Smith, of whom we sing "oh, what rapture filled his bosom, For he saw the living God."[7]

England, ever conciliatory, thought that Mormon writers can and should satisfy both sets of criteria. The content of Mormon literature, he wrote, should reflect the *full* experience of Mormonism, including the difficult and the tragic, and should not descend to didactic affirmation of Mormon doctrine. Nevertheless, it can resist secularization—particularly by "stand[ing] firm against secular man's increasing skepticism about the efficacy of language to get at the irreducible otherness of things outside the mind, to make sense, and beauty, of that 'chaotic matter which is element.'"[8] Moreover, he wrote,

> if Mormon writers take seriously the fact that language is a gift from God, the creator, that gives them access to the "glory" that dwells in matter and in other intelligences, including God's, they can confidently use language, not like others merely to imitate (albeit with compassionate despair) the separated, meaningless, raw elements and experience of a doomed universe, but to create genuinely new things, verbal structures of element and intelligence and experience that include understanding and judgment as well as imitation and empathy. We can,

like our contemporaries, create of words what Wallace Stevens called "things that do not exist without the words. . . ."[9]

The essay works to situate Mormon literature from various periods between the poles of "orthodox didacticism and faithful realism." England warns that "the future of Mormon literature is potentially both bright and vexed." He saw vexation in the increasingly bifurcated and partisan divides between journals and forums where LDS literature was being presented and published. Nevertheless, the essay ends as it began, with earnest optimism, and also with England's characteristic emphasis on literature as a communal project involving the audience as well as the author:

> We must be willing, both as writers and readers, to do as Joseph Smith did—and called us to do: "Thy mind, . . . if thou wilt lead a soul unto salvation, must stretch as high as the utmost heavens, and search into and contemplate the darkest abyss, and the broad expanse of eternity." A literature to match the high religious achievement of the restoration Joseph Smith began requires both the breadth and the depth he achieved—literary skill, moral courage, and generosity—and also the spiritual passion that brought about his visions and continues to give a unique quality to the life of faithful Mormons.[10]

England elaborates on the dangers of bifurcation between those who prize orthodoxy and those who prioritize artistic achievement in a 1999 review essay titled "Danger on the Right! Danger on the Left! The Ethics of Recent Mormon Fiction." The essay is a review of two volumes of LDS fiction, *Turning Hearts: Short Stories on Family Life*, published by Bookcraft, a quasi-official imprint of the LDS Church, and *In Our Lovely Deseret: Mormon Fictions*, published by Signature Books, a militantly independent and unofficial publisher whose work generally appealed to Mormon and Mormon-adjacent readers who did not necessarily require orthodoxy as a principal criterion for literature. England characterizes the writing of the first collection as cautious, pious, and amateur, and the second as liberal, experimental, and aggressively impious. His thesis is that, despite these surface differences, the stories in both books fail for similar aesthetic and ethical reasons. The editors of both collections, writes England, "coming from very different places, seem to indulge in the same fallacy—that good ethical fiction can be produced by mere commitment to ethical positions, by an ideological design, one that is either already in favor of certain didactic premises or already against them, with either a right-wing or a left-wing cultural agenda. That leads directly to ethical manipulation, not ethical discovery and genuine change."[11] It is instructive to note England's use of "right-wing" and "left-wing" here, the way that terms from American politics and culture wars are mapped onto questions of Mormon orthodoxy. The collapse of political, cultural, artistic, and religious categories is characteristic of the dangerous bifurcation England is decrying in this essay. The fact that England himself slides into using this vocabulary points to the difficulty of escaping these cultural categories and of extricating Mormon debates from their American context; the essay both diagnoses and performs the problem. England's prescription is, characteristically, maturity and hard work. After going through infelicitous examples from the two flawed collections he is reviewing, he cites older Mormon literature that avoids the treacly sentimentality and didactic orthodoxy of Bookcraft's anthology, and the self-righteous and equally didactic condemnation of that orthodoxy in the Signature Books' collection.

From the Bookcraft anthology, he mentions Virginia Sorenson's story, "Where Nothing Is Long Ago," Levi Peterson's "The Confessions of Augustine," and Douglas Thayer's "Opening Day." All three stories deal in varying contexts with the Mormon (and Western) tendency to resort to and even celebrate needless violence. All three are narrated from the perspective of older people recalling incidents from their youth. And all three, according to England, offer "a more devastating and a more compassionate critique of Mormon culture" than the heavy-handed criticisms in Signature Books' anthology. Ultimately, he says these stories also more effectively bear witness to the truths of Mormonism than the stories in the Bookcraft anthology that have testimony as their primary goal:

> The chief formal tool of an ethical storyteller, I believe, is the skillful use of point of view, especially first person or implied persona, to communicate powerfully to the reader both intense sympathy for the characters and also various means of evaluating their moral journeys. . . . Sorensen reminds us of all this, subtly, with her skillful use of complex point of view, and then she ends her essay with a reversal of roles, the naive child confronting the horror and the mature woman showing her compassion for the "other" in her determination to write about her own people's strange but understandable ways. She both increases our ethical judgment of wrong and our empathy for those who are wrong.[12]

Taken together, these two essays provide an overview of Mormon literary history through the end of the twentieth century, and a guide to the particularly Mormon mode of literary criticism practiced by one of its foremost critics and champions.

England, Eugene. "The Achievement of Lowell Bennion." *Sunstone* 12.4 (Jul. 1988): 24–30.

———. "Beyond 'Jack-Fiction.'" Review of Levi Peterson's *The Backslider*, Linda Sillitoe's *Sideways to the Sun*, and Orson Scott Card's *Seventh Son. BYU Studies* 28.2 (Summer 1988): 110–20.

———. "Born Square: On Being Mormon, Western, and Human." *Literature and Belief* 21.1 (2001): 275–94.

———. "Creative Writing 101." Review of Mary Morris's *Crossroads* and Chuck Wachtel's *Joe the Engineer. Chronicles of Culture* 7.10 (Oct. 1983): 22–23.

———. "Danger on the Right! Danger on the Left!: The Ethics of Recent Mormon Fiction." *Dialogue: A Journal of Mormon Thought* 32.3 (Fall 1999): 13–30.

———. "Douglas Thayer's *Mr. Wahlquist in Yellowstone: A Mormon's Christian Response to Wilderness." BYU Studies* 34.1 (1994): 52–72.

———. "*Faithful Fiction.*" Review of Douglas Thayer's *Summer Fire, Greening Wheat: Fifteen Mormon Short Stories*, edited by Levi Peterson; and Donald Marshall's *Zinnie Stokes. Dialogue: A Journal of Mormon Thought* 18.4 (Winter 1985): 196–201.

———. "Good Literature for a Chosen People." *Dialogue: A Journal of Mormon Thought* 39.1 (Spring 1999): 69–89.

———. "How Mormon Women Figure Things Out." Review of Mary Lythgoe Bradford's *Mormon Women Speak: A Collection of Essays. Sunstone* 3.4/5 (Apr./May 1983): 29–31.

———. "Hugh Nibley as Cassandra." Review of vols. 7 and 9 of *The Collected Works of Hugh Nibley, Since Cumorah* and *Approaching Zion* and *Warfare in the Book of Mormon*, edited by Stephen D. Ricks and William J. Hamblin. *BYU Studies* 30.4 (Fall 1990): 104–16.

———. "Modern Acts of the Apostles, 1840: Mormon Literature in the Making." *BYU Studies* 27.2 (1987): 1–17.

———. "Only the Best We Have: Capitalism and the Divine Economics. . . ." Review of *The Spirit of Democratic Capitalism*, by Michael Novak. *Sunstone* 2.1 (1982): 25–28.

———. "Playing Pointless Games." Review of *Literacy and the Survival of Humanism, by.* Richard A. Lanham. *Chronicles of Culture* 9.10 (Oct. 1985): 27–28.

———. Review of *A Believing People: Literature of the Latter-day Saints*, edited by Richard H. Cracroft and Neal E. Lambert. *BYU Studies* 15.3 (Spring 1975): 365–72.

———. Review of *The Canyons of Grace*, by Levi Peterson. *BYU Studies* 23.1 (Winter 1983): 33–38.

———. Review of *God's Fools: Plays of Mitigated Conscience*, by Thomas F. Rogers. *BYU Studies* 26.2 (Summer 1986): 115–18.

———. Review of *Mr. Wahlquist in Yellowstone*, by Douglas Thayer. *Western American Literature* 25.1 (Spring 1990): 51–53.

———. Review of *Night Soil*, by Levi Peterson. *Weber Studies* 8.2 (Fall 1991): 99–100.

———. Review of *Pastwatch: The Redemption of Christopher Columbus*, by Orson Scott Card. *Association for Mormon Letters Review Site.* http://www.aml-online.org/Reviews/.

———, ed. *Bright Angels and Familiars: Contemporary Mormon Stories.* Salt Lake City: Signature Books, 1992.

England, Eugene, and Lavina Fielding Anderson, eds. *Tending the Garden: Essays on Mormon Literature.* Salt Lake City: Signature Books, 1996.

England, Eugene, and Dennis Clark, eds. *Harvest: Contemporary Mormon Poems.* Salt Lake City: Signature Books, 1989.

England, Eugene, and Charles D. Tate Jr. "On Being Human and Being a Prophet." Review of *Spencer W. Kimball*, by Edward L. Kimball and Andrew E. Kimball Jr. *BYU Studies* 18.4 (Summer 1978): 591–98.

Pacifism

Although his commitment to dialogue and proving contraries compelled him to acknowledge the components of just war theory in the Book of Mormon, England almost always came down on the pacifist side of the dilemma. He traced his turn toward more liberal political views to his disillusionment over the government's lies about the Gulf of Tonkin incident during the war in Vietnam, and was generally skeptical of American military intervention abroad.

The most comprehensive articulation of England's pacifism is in a chapter in the 1995 book *Making Peace*. In the chapter titled "Thou Shalt Not Kill," England grounds a Mormon ethic first in the Pentateuch's "Thou shalt not kill" and in the Doctrine and Covenants' elaboration of that command: "Thou shalt not kill or do anything like unto it." Christ's command to "love your enemies" is invoked, as well as the Pauline injunction to "overcome evil with good." Finally, he draws on the Mormon doctrine of eternal intelligences to amplify the Levinasian demand of the other who meets our gaze to be treated as an end in herself. The conclusion he draws is perhaps the most absolute of any of his expressed convictions:

> A Mormon theology of life then is based, I believe, on an absolute ethic, grounded in the right and need of all humans to treat and be treated as humans. War, violence of any kind, including torture, physical punishment, abortion for convenience, and capital punishment, violate that right and consequently dehumanize the objects, the perpetrators, and the society that condones that violence.[13]

An earlier essay, "Why Nephi Killed Laban: Reflections on the Truth of the Book of Mormon," uses René Girard's theories about mimetic violence to read this episode. The essay's focus is on ways that reading the Book of Mormon as literature can help show its truthfulness and value, but it also illustrates England's essentially pacifist reading of the Book of Mormon. "The Book of Mormon is quite consistent," he writes, ". . . with Girard's very helpful focus on the Atonement as achieved through love rather than through traditional sacrifice, through reconciliation rather than payment."

Other essays respond to contemporary conflicts in Vietnam, Iraq, and to nuclear weapons projects in the United States.

England, Eugene. "Late Night Thoughts at the End of a War." *Dialogue: A Journal of Mormon Thought* 24.2 (Summer 1991): 7–9.
———. *Making Peace: Personal Essays.* Salt Lake City: Signature Books, 1995.
———. "On Trusting God, or Why We Should Not Fight Iraq." *Sunstone* 14.5 (Oct. 1990): 9–12.
———. "Thou Shalt Not Kill." In *Making Peace: Personal Essays,* 157–75. Salt Lake City: Signature Books, 1995.
———. "The Tragedy of Vietnam and the Responsibility of Mormons." *Dialogue: A Journal of Mormon Thought* 2.4 (Winter 1967): 71–91.
———. "What Covenant Will God Receive in the Desert?" *Sunstone* 17.2 (Sept. 1994): 26–34.
———. "Why Nephi Killed Laban: Reflections on the Truth of the Book of Mormon." *Dialogue: A Journal of Mormon Thought* 22.3 (Fall 1989): 32–51.

Race

England's engagement with issues of race in the LDS Church is well known. The proscription forbidding Black members of the church from being ordained to the priesthood or receiving temple endowments was a critical issue facing Mormons in the United States in the years when England was in graduate school, and it was for him personally a continuing source of anguish. *Dialogue*'s most controversial and influential volumes were those addressing LDS policy and doctrine about race. In "The Mormon Cross," England theorized that the priesthood and temple rites were being withheld from Black members of the church not because *they* had done anything wrong in pre-Earth life, as some Mormons had taught, but because white Latter-day Saints were racist and needed to repent before God's will could be done and the priesthood and temple rites extended to all of God's children.

England made two especially important contributions in the lead-up to the lifting of the ban. First, as editor of *Dialogue*, he published Armand Mauss's 1967 article, "Mormonism and the Negro: Faith, Folklore, and Civil Rights." He praised Lester Bush's 1973 "Mormonism's Negro Doctrine: An Historical Overview," also published in *Dialogue*, which was especially important in documenting the historical origins of the policy and also the fact that the policy *preceded* the doctrine that supposedly justified it. Second, England focused from the beginning not only on the fact of the priesthood and temple restriction, but also on the official and unofficial "doctrine" that had been adduced to justify it. He rightly saw that changing the practice was only part of undoing the problem.

After the 1978 announcement that the priesthood and temple rites would no longer be restricted, England continued to speak out against lingering racism among church members and against the various explanatory theologies that church leaders and educators had invented for the practice. He often quoted Apostle Bruce R. McConkie's statement repudiating his own teachings justifying the policy. In a beautiful and humble reversal of his prior teachings, McConkie had said:

> I would like to say something about the new revelation relative to the priesthood going to those of all nations and races. "He [meaning Christ, who is the Lord God] inviteth them all to come unto him and partake of his goodness; and he denieth none that come unto him, black and white, bond and free, male and female; and he remembereth the heathen; and all are alike unto God, both Jew and Gentile" (2 Nephi 26:33).
>
> These words have now taken on a new meaning. We have caught a new vision of their true significance. . . . Many of us never imagined or supposed that they had the extensive and broad meaning that they do have.

. . . There are statements in our literature by the early Brethren which we have interpreted to mean that the Negroes would not receive the priesthood in mortality. I have said the same things. . . .

Forget everything that I have said, or what President Brigham Young or President George Q. Cannon or whomsoever has said in days past that is contrary to the present revelation. We spoke with a limited understanding and without the light and knowledge that now has come into the world.[14]

This statement, however, was made in a speech at BYU, not to the general membership of the church, so the efforts of England (and others) to make sure it became more widely known were critical. As late as 1998, England was lamenting the fact that many of his students—most of them, even— still believed racist ideas and doctrines that had been taught in the fifties, sixties, and seventies:

I check occasionally in classes at BYU and find that still, twenty years after the revelation, a majority of bright, well-educated Mormon students say they believe that Blacks are descendants of Cain and Ham and thereby cursed and that skin color is an indication of righteousness in the pre-mortal life. They tell me these ideas came from their parents or Seminary and Sunday School teachers, and they have never questioned them.[15]

England wrote that these beliefs could be as damning to white Mormons as their earlier racist practice, that these teachings would prevent the growth of the LDS Church on Earth and, worse, would prevent members who believed them from fully understanding and experiencing the love of God: "All human beings *must* be alike unto God and we *must* understand that that is *true* for the plan of salvation to work—for faith unto repentance, the experience of Christ's Atonement, and exaltation even to be possible." England's prescience in understanding that it would be harder to change minds than policy made him an important, effective, and remarkably persistent advocate over many decades.

England, Eugene. "Are All Alike unto God?: Prejudice against Blacks and Women in Popular Mormon Thought." *Sunstone* 15.2 (Mar./Apr. 1990): 21–31.
———. "Combatting Racism and Sexism at BYU: An Open Letter to Faculty and Students." *Student Review* 4.3 (4 Oct. 1989): 10.
———. "'Lamanites' and the Spirit of the Lord." *Dialogue: A Journal of Mormon Thought* 18.4 (Winter 1985): 25–32.

———. "The Mormon Cross." *Dialogue: A Journal of Mormon Thought* 8.1 (Spring 1973): 78–86.

Poetry

England was not a prolific poet, but he did publish poems throughout his life. Most were published in Mormon periodicals: *Dialogue, BYU Studies, Sunstone,* and *Exponent II.* Several poems are online at http://www.eugeneengland.org/selected-writings/poetry.

One of his earliest published poems—evidently influenced by Dylan Thomas—was in the first issue of *Dialogue*:

> The Firegiver
> God, forgive my pen its trespass,
> And I forgive thee the sweet burning
> That drives it on through thy dominion.
>
> God, if what it might encompass,
> If shapes of love, thy face, or being
> Itself are challenged in its question,
>
> Indulge the hand that ventures into flame,
> Suffer my searching, for you share the blame.

One of his best poems, "Kinsman," memorializes the episode with his father praying to consecrate the wheat harvest, which England always cited as one of the defining moments of his life and faith. The final stanzas read:

> Plucking random heads, we counted and chewed
> The milky kernels. And then he knelt,
> Still grasping the wheat, in fierce repose.
> I stood and watched his face. He said:
>
> "Thou art the Prince who holds my heart
> And gives my body power to make.
> The fruit is thine: this wheat, this boy;
> Protect the yield that we may live!"
>
> And fear thrilled me on that hushed ground,
> So that I grew beyond the wheat
> And watched my father take his hold
> On what endures behind the veil.

In his review of *Harvest: Contemporary Mormon Poems*, a collection edited by England and Dennis Clark, Richard Cracroft cites this poem as an example of fully realized *Mormon* art (as compared to other poems that he feels are technically skillful, but earthbound and not especially Mormon).[16] Later, in a memorial tribute to England, Cracroft offered further praise: "Tenacious in argument, convinced in belief, clear in discourse, his work, in whatever genre he chooses, seems all of a piece, and even a casual reading of his poetry suggests that these qualities are recognizable in the lamentably few pieces available to us. His poems are admirably direct and shapely, and move firmly toward their intended last lines. They have a planned certainty about them, a confidence."[17]

England's poetry is almost always thematically Mormon. It also almost always includes family relationships, and frequently situates those relationships in nature. A poem for Charlotte is one of the last things he wrote in his final illness. It is a slightly awkward poem, and a perfect final offering.

Your Comfort Close By
   A Poem by Gene for Charlotte
   Mother's Day, 2001
I woke to hear you breathing next to me
And knew you'd wakened often in the night
To help in what is now my being's fight
To stay alive and get my body free
Of cancer and paralysis. I knew
You'd wake again to help: read me to sleep
Or rise to fix me healing food and keep
Me clean and warm and dressed—or teach me not to rue
My life.

We talked of all we'd forged together—home
And children, faith and vows that make us one—
And all we still might make in Kingdoms where
None can sever us from continued seed forever
Or me from your comfort close by.

Notes

Chapter 1. Eugene England

1. Eugene England, "'No Cause, No Cause': An Essay toward Reconciliation," *Sunstone* 121 (Jan. 2002): 31.

2. Matthew Bowman, *The Mormon People: The Making of an American Faith* (New York: Random House, 2012), 164–66.

3. Doctrine and Covenants 130:19.

4. Eugene England, *Dialogues with Myself* (Midvale, UT: Signature Books, 1984), 191.

5. Ibid., 194.

6. Eugene England, *Why the Church Is as True as the Gospel* (Salt Lake City: Bookcraft, 1986), 1.

7. Bert Wilson, "Recollections of 'Eugene,'" http://www.eugeneengland.org/eugene-england/remembering-gene-project/remembering-gene/recollections-of-eugene, accessed 30 Jan. 2020.

8. Ibid.

9. Alan Brown, "An Unlikely Friendship," http://www.eugeneengland.org/eugene-england/remembering-gene-project/remembering-gene/an-unlikely-friendship, accessed 30 Jan. 2020.

10. Jim McMichael, "Conversations!" http://www.eugeneengland.org/eugene-england/remembering-gene-project/remembering-gene-mission-marriage-mit-air-force-stanford-dialogue/conversations, accessed 30 Jan. 2020.

11. Floyd Astin, "A Few Memories of My Friend Eugene England," http://www.eugeneengland.org/eugene-england/remembering-gene-project/remembering-gene/a-few-memories-of-my-friend-eugene-england, accessed 30 Jan. 2020.

12. David E. Harris, Interview with Charlotte England, 29 Dec. 2015, http://wasatchhollowcc.org/index.php/charlotte-hawkins-england, accessed 2 Feb. 2020; John Gary Maxwell, "Four Friends," http://www.eugeneengland.org/

eugene-england/remembering-gene-project/remembering-gene/four-friends, accessed 2 Feb. 2020.

13. The LDS Institute is the program run by the LDS Church Educational System for college-age students to receive religious instruction alongside their secular education. In many places, the classes are held in church buildings; in places with large LDS student populations, like Utah universities, the Institute often has a dedicated building for classes and gatherings.

14. Eugene England, "The Achievement of Lowell Bennion," *Sunstone* 12.4 (Jul. 1988): 26.

15. Ibid.

16. Quoted in Eugene England, *The Best of Lowell Bennion* (Salt Lake City: Deseret Book, 1988), Kindle edition, chap. 7

17. Quoted in ibid.

18. The Church Education System is the department of the centralized church administration responsible for teaching Mormon youth in Seminary and Institutes of Religion—for high school and college students, respectively.

19. Eugene England, "Mission to Paradise," *BYU Studies* 38.1 (1999): 178.

20. Ibid., 182–83.

21. Jack Adamson, "Fulbright to India," https://jackadamsonproject.blog/category/history-of-ideas-2/, accessed 20 Feb. 2020.

22. Bonnie Dalton, Kate Handley, and Ken Handley, "Snapshots from New England and Beyond," http://www.eugeneengland.org/eugene-england/remembering-gene-project/remembering-gene-mission-marriage-mit-air-force-stanford-dialogue/snapshots-from-new-england-and-beyond, accessed 30 Jan. 2020; Claudia Bushman et al., "Brattle Street Elegy," *Dialogue: A Journal of Mormon Thought* 42.4 (Winter 2009): 139–48.

23. Jerry Cannon, http://www.eugeneengland.org/eugene-england/remembering-gene-project/remembering-gene-mission-marriage-mit-air-force-stanford-dialogue/gene-in-service, accessed 30 Jan. 2020.

24. England, "'No Cause, No Cause,'" 32.

25. Ibid.

26. Articles of Faith 12, Pearl of Great Price.

27. Eugene England, interview by Davis Bitton, 16 Nov. 1975, Salt Lake City, UT, https://catalog.churchofjesuschrist.org/record?id=e8d2c16d-92b3-4218-bc82-4804621d7375&view=summary. Transcript at eugeneengland.org/wp-content/uploads/sbi/articles/1975_sc_op_004.pdf, accessed 8 Apr. 2021.

28. Correspondence from Eugene England to Marion Hanks, 21 Mar. 1974, Accn 2426, box 171, folder 9, Eugene England Papers 1825–2003, Special Collections and Archives, University of Utah, J. Willard Marriott, Salt Lake City, UT.

29. Ray and Jeanne Jacobsen, "Lifting Our Thinking," http://www.eugene england.org/eugene-england/remembering-gene-project/st-olaf-college-to -early-byu-career/lifting-our-thinking, accessed 8 Apr. 2021.

30. Eugene England, *Brother Brigham* (Salt Lake City: Bookcraft, 1980).

31. England, *Why the Church Is as True as the Gospel*, 94.

32. Ibid., 95.

33. Eugene England, "Knowledge without Zeal," a statement on honors education at BYU given to the Humanities College faculty, 7 Dec. 1978, eugene england.org/wp-content/uploads/sbi/articles/1978_sc_op_004.pdf.

34. Tim Slover, "In Joy and Bliss to Be Me By: How Gene Was in London," http://www.eugeneengland.org/eugene-england/remembering-gene-project/ gene-in-england/in-joy-and-bliss-to-be-me-by-how-gene-was-in-london, accessed 30 Jan. 2020.

35. Gordon B. Hinckley, "Daughters of God," address to the General Conference of the Church of Jesus Christ of Latter-day Saints, October 1991, https:// www.churchofjesuschrist.org/study/general-conference/1991/10/daughters-of -god?lang=eng, accessed 10 Feb. 2020.

36. Bryan Waterman and Brian Kagel, *The Lord's University* (Salt Lake City: Signature Books, 1998), 203–13.

37. Eugene England, "Let's Renounce the Remaining Racism," *Student Review* 3.18 (1 Feb. 1989): 6–7.

38. Eugene England, "Prior Restraint and Guilt by Association: Reflections on Academic Freedom at BYU," *Student Review* 3.28 (12 Apr. 1989): 3; reprinted in "The Year in Review" issue, 4.1 (20 Sept. 1989): 15.

39. Eugene England, "Combatting Racism and Sexism at BYU: An Open Letter to Faculty and Students," *Student Review* 4.3 (4 Oct. 1989): 10.

40. Dallin H. Oaks and Russell M. Nelson, cited in Bryan Waterman and Brian Kagel, *The Lord's University* (Salt Lake City: Signature Books, 1998), http://signaturebookslibrary.org/the-lords-university-05/, accessed 10 Feb. 2020.

41. Boyd K. Packer, "Talk to the All-Church Coordinating Council," 18 May 1993, https://www.zionsbest.com/face.html.

42. Eugene England, "On Spectral Evidence," *Dialogue* 26.1 (Spring 1993): 140.

43. England, "'No Cause, No Cause,'" 31–39.

44. Brian Birch, "Between Scylla and Charybdis: Championing Mormon Studies at Utah Valley State College," *Sunstone* 121 (Jan. 2002): 49.

45. Correspondence from Eugene England to Neal Maxwell, 16 Jan. 2001, Accn 2426, box 171, folder 9, Eugene England Papers 1825–2003.

46. Correspondence from Neal Maxwell to Eugene England, 25 Jan. 2001, Accn 2426, box 171, folder 9, Eugene England Papers 1825–2003.

Chapter 2. Toward Integrity

1. Eugene England, *Dialogues with Myself* (Midvale, UT: Signature Books, 1984),

2. Ibid., 196.

3. Paul Tillich, *The Courage to Be*, 3rd ed. (New Haven: Yale University Press, 2014), 34.

4. Ibid., 51.

5. England, *Dialogues with Myself*, 196.

6. Ibid., 203.

7. England, *Dialogues with Myself*, 48.

8. Eugene England, *Why the Church Is as True as the Gospel* (Salt Lake City: Bookcraft, 1986), 110.

9. Ibid., 112.

10. Ibid., 115.

11. Quoted in ibid., 122.

12. Talal Asad, *Genealogies of Religion* (Baltimore: Johns Hopkins University Press, 1993), 138.

13. James K. A. Smith, *Desiring the Kingdom (Cultural Liturgies): Worship, Worldview, and Cultural Formation* (Grand Rapids, MI: Baker Academic, 2009), 18.

14. Jack Adamson, "The Great Soul," *Journal of the Maharaja Sayajiro University of Baroda Gandhi Centenary* 18.1/2 (Apr./Jul. 1969), https://jackadamson project.blog/2015/07/23/the-great-soul/, accessed 10 Feb. 2020.

15. John A. Widtsoe, *A Rational Theology, as Taught by the Church of Jesus Christ of Latter-day Saints* (Salt Lake City: Deseret Book, 1937), 178–79.

16. Ibid., 142.

17. William James, *Manuscript Lectures* (Cambridge, MA: Harvard University Press, 1988), liii–liv.

18. Correspondence from John Widtsoe to Jacob Trayner, 8 Oct. 1934, CR 712/2, box 38, folder 6, John A. Widtsoe Papers, Church History Library, The Church of Jesus Christ of Latter-day Saints, Salt Lake City, UT. I am indebted to Ardis E. Parshall for making me aware of this letter.

19. William James, *The Will to Believe and Other Essays in Popular Philosophy* (New York: Dover Publications, 1966), 24.

20. England, *Why the Church Is as True as the Gospel*, 3.

21. Ibid.

22. Ibid., 4.

23. Ibid., 5.

24. Ibid., 7.

25. Ibid., 11.

26. Ibid., 13.

27. Ibid., 14.

28. Eugene England, "The Lord's University?," Accn 2426, box 54, folder 5, Eugene England Papers 1825–2003, Special Collections and Archives, University of Utah, J. Willard Marriott, Salt Lake City, UT.

29. Stanley Thayne, "Pragmatizing Mormonism and Baptizing William James," *Juvenile Instructor* (blog), 23 Feb. 2008, https://juvenileinstructor.org/pragmatizing-mormonism-and-baptizing-william-james-or-was-william-james-a-closet-mormon-and-joseph-smith-a-proto-pragmatist-part-i-on-william-james-and-mormonism/, accessed 18 Nov. 2020.

30. Eugene England, Review of *A Believing People: Literature of the Latter-day Saints*, ed. Richard H. Cracroft and Neal E. Lambert, *BYU Studies* 15.3 (Spring 1975): 370.

31. England, *Dialogues with Myself*, x.

32. Eugene England, "Great Books or True Religion: Defining the Mormon Scholar," *Dialogue: A Journal of Mormon Thought* 9.4 (Winter 1974): 39.

33. Ibid., 41.

34. Ibid., 46–47.

35. Eugene England, "A Modern Acts of the Apostles, 1840: Mormon Literature in the Making," *BYU Studies* 27.2 (1987): 16.

36. Ibid., 14.

37. Eugene England, *Converted to Christ through the Book of Mormon* (Salt Lake City: Deseret Book, 1989).

38. Eugene England and Robert Rees, eds., *The Reader's Book of Mormon* (Salt Lake City: Signature Books, 2008), ix.

39. Jack Adamson, undated lecture notes, https://jackadamsonproject.blog/2015/07/14/how-writers-use-the-bible/, accessed 3 Mar. 2020.

40. Eugene England, "Why Nephi Killed Laban: Reflections on the Truth of the Book of Mormon," *Dialogue: A Journal of Mormon Thought* 22.3 (Fall 1989): 32.

41. Ibid., 34.

42. Ibid., 36–37.

43. Pierre Bourdieu, *Distinction: Social Critique of the Judgement of Taste*, trans. R. Nice (Cambridge, MA: Harvard University Press and Routledge & Kegan Paul, 1984), 4–5.

44. Friedrich Schiller, "On Grace and Dignity," in *Letters on Aesthetic Education, Schillers Werke, Nationalausgabe*, ed. Julius Petersen et al. (Weimar: Hermann Böhlaus Nachfolger, 1943–2013), 20:255, cited in Jane V. Curran and Christophe Fricker, eds., *Schiller's "On Grace and Dignity" in Its Cultural Context: Essays and a New Translation* (Rochester, NY: Camden House, 2005), 127.

45. Eugene England, *The Quality of Mercy* (Salt Lake City: Bookcraft, 1992), 7.

46. Eugene England, "My Kinsman, Major Molineux," *Literature and Belief* 3 (1983): 119.

47. Book of Mormon, 1 Nephi 19:23.

48. Eugene England, "'No Cause, No Cause': An Essay toward Reconciliation," *Sunstone* 121 (Jan. 2002): 36.

49. "Great Books or True Religion," 39.

50. Susan Taber, quoted in Gideon O. Burton, " The Literary Legacy of Eugene England," *Irreantum* 3.3 (Autumn 2001): 6.

51. Richard H. Cracroft and Neal E. Lambert, eds., *A Believing People: Literature of the Latter-day Saints* (Salt Lake City: Deseret Book, 1979), foreword.

52. Ibid.

53. England, Review of *A Believing People*, 370.

54. Cracroft and Lambert, *A Believing People*, foreword.

55. England, Review of *A Believing People*, 370.

56. Ibid.

57. Mary Lythgoe Bradford, "I, Eye, Aye: A Personal Essay on Personal Essays," in *Tending the Garden*, ed. England and Anderson, 147–60.

58. Burton, "The Literary Legacy of Eugene England," 6.

59. England, *Dialogues with Myself*, 183–84.

60. Eugene England, "On Being Male and Melchizedek," *Dialogue: A Journal of Mormon Thought* 23.4 (Winter 1990): 75.

Chapter 3. The Possibilities of Dialogue

1. Eugene England, "Healing and Making Peace in the Church and the World," in *Making Peace: Personal Essays (Salt Lake City: Signature Books, 1995)*, chap. 1, http://signaturebookslibrary.org/healing-and-making-peace-in-the-church-and-the-world/.

2. As part of their tradition of lay clergy, Latter-day Saints take turns giving homilies (which are called "talks" in the Mormon vernacular) in Sunday services; there is no regular preacher.

3. Eugene England, "'No Cause, No Cause': An Essay toward Reconciliation," *Sunstone* 121 (Jan. 2002): 31–39.

4. Book of Mormon, 2 Nephi 2:11–13.

5. Eugene England, *Why the Church Is as True as the Gospel* (Salt Lake City: Bookcraft, 1986), 2–3.

6. England, *Making Peace*, 90.

7. Peter Crawley, "Parley E. Pratt: Father of Mormon Pamphleteering," *Dialogue: A Journal of Mormon Thought* 15.3 (Fall 1982): 13.

8. Mario De Pillis, "The Quest for Religious Authority and the Rise of Mormonism," *Dialogue: A Journal of Mormon Thought* 1.1 (Spring 1966): 88.

9. Richard Haglund and David Whittaker, "Intellectual History," in *Encyclopedia of Mormonism*, vol. 2, ed. Daniel H. Ludlow (New York: Macmillan, 1992), 438, https://eom.byu.edu/index.php?title=Intellectual_History&oldid=4649, accessed 10 Feb. 2020.

10. Russel B. Swensen, "Mormons at the University of Chicago Divinity School, a Personal Reminiscence," *Dialogue: A Journal of Mormon Thought* 7.2 (Summer 1972): 41.

11. Ibid., 42.

12. Gary James Bergera and Ronald Priddis, "The Organic Evolution Controversy," *in Brigham Young University: A House of Faith* (Salt Lake City: Signature Books, 1985), 131–71.

13. Quoted in Thomas Simpson, *American Universities and the Birth of Mormon Mormonism 1867–1940* (Chapel Hill: University of North Carolina Press, 2016), 115–16.

14. Edward A. Geary, "Mormondom's Lost Generation: The Novelists of the 1940s," *BYU Studies Quarterly* 18:1, January 1978, 89.

15. Thomas Alexander, *Mormonism in Transition: A History of the Latter-day Saints, 1890–1930* (Urbana: University of Illinois Press, 1996), 152.

16. Matthew Bowman, *The Mormon People* (New York: Random House, 2012), 195.

17. Tina Hatch, "'Changing Times Bring Changing Conditions': Relief Society 1960–the Present," *Dialogue: A Journal of Mormon Thought* 37.3 (Fall 2004): 73.

18 Devery Anderson, "A History of *Dialogue*, Part One: The Early Years, 1965–1971," *Dialogue: A Journal of Mormon Thought* 32.2 (Summer 1999): 16n7.

19. Ibid., 17–18.

20. Ibid., 21.

21. Ibid.

22. Ibid., 23n38.

23. Letter from Hugh Nibley to Chauncey Riddle, 29 Oct. 1963, cited in Boyd Jay Petersen, *Hugh Nibley: A Consecrated Life* (Salt Lake City: Greg Kofford Books, 2002), 304n72.

24. Ibid.

25. Quoted in Anderson, "A History of *Dialogue*, Part One," 26.

26. Quoted in ibid., 36.

27. Marian Ashby Johnson and Wesley Johnson, "On the Trail of the Twentieth-Century Mormon Outmigration," *Brigham Young University Studies* 46.1 (2007): 64.

28 Latter-day Saints conceive of themselves as having been adopted into the House of Israel, and sometimes refer to non-Mormons as "Gentiles." In the late twentieth and twenty-first centuries, this usage is often somewhat tongue in cheek, but it is supported by earnestly believed doctrine.

29. Johnson and Johnson, "On the Trail of the Twentieth-Century Mormon Outmigration," 56.

30. Correspondence from Marion Hanks to Eugene England, 13 Sept. 1965, Accn 2426, box 171, folder 9, Eugene England Papers, Special Collections and Archives, University of Utah, J. Willard Marriott, Salt Lake City, UT.

31. Correspondence from Eugene England to Marion Hanks, 4 Nov. 1965, Accn 2426, box 171, folder 9, Eugene England Papers.

32. Correspondence from Marion Hanks to Eugene England, 4 Oct. 1968, Accn 2426, box 171, folder 9, Eugene England Papers.

33. Correspondence from Marion Hanks to Eugene England, 14 Nov. 1969, Accn 2426, box 171, folder 9, Eugene England Papers.

34. Correspondence from Neal A. Maxwell to Eugene England, 28 Feb. 1968, Accn 2426, box 171, folder 18, Eugene England Papers.

35. Correspondence from Eugene England to Neal A. Maxwell, 30 June 1970, Accn 2426, box 171, folder 18, Eugene England Papers.

36. Correspondence from Neal Maxwell to Eugene England, 6 Jul. 1970, Accn 2426, box 171, folder 18, Eugene England Papers.

37. Correspondence from Eugene England to Neal A. Maxwell, 17 Sept. 1994, Accn 2426, box 171, folder 18, Eugene England Papers.

38. England, *Making Peace*, 35.

39. Transcript of McConkie remarks, cited in Rebecca England, "A Professor and Apostle Correspond," http://www.eugeneengland.org/a-professor-and-apostle-correspond-eugene-england-and-bruce-r-mcconkie-on-the-nature-of-god.

40. Bruce R. McConkie, "The Seven Deadly Heresies," *BYU Devotional*, 1 June 1980, https://speeches.byu.edu/talks/bruce-r-mcconkie/seven-deadly-heresies/.

41. Correspondence from Eugene England to Bruce McConkie, Sept. 1980, http://www.eugeneengland.org/wp-content/uploads/2012/07/EE-to-BRM-Sep-80-Combined.pdf.

42. Brigham Young, *Journal of Discourses*, 11:286, cited in Eugene England, "Perfection and Progression: Two Complementary Ways to Talk about God," *BYU Studies* 29.3 (Summer 1989): 37.

43. Ibid., 38.

44. Ibid.

45. Doctrine and Covenants, 1835, [12], Joseph Smith Papers, https://www .josephsmithpapers.org/paper-summary/doctrine-and-covenants-1835/20, accessed 26 Mar. 2020.

46. Ibid., 26.

47. Joseph Fielding Smith, *Doctrines of Salvation: Sermons and Writings of Joseph Fielding Smith*, compiled by Bruce R. McConkie (Salt Lake City: Bookcraft, 1972), 7–8.

48. John A. Widtsoe, cited in England, "Perfection and Progression," 41. Emphasis added by England.

49. Brigham Young, cited in England, "Perfection and Progression," 43. Emphasis added by England.

50. Correspondence from Bruce R. McConkie to Eugene England, 19 Feb. 1981, www.eugeneengland.org/wp-content/uploads/2012/07/BRM-to-EE-Feb -80-Combined.pdf.

51. Mormon vernacular for scripture.

52. Joseph Smith et al., *History of the Church of Jesus Christ of Latter-day Saints*, ed. B. H. Roberts, 7 vols., 2d ed. rev. (Salt Lake City: Deseret Book, 1948), 5:339–40.

53. Young, *Journal of Discourses*, 9:150.

54. Latter-day Saint doctrine holds that human beings will be judged and assigned to one of three kingdoms in the afterlife (rather than simply to heaven or hell, as in other traditions).

55. Correspondence from Neal A. Maxwell to Reed Durham, undated, Accn 2426, box 171, folder 18, Eugene England Papers.

56. Bowman, *Mormon People*, 195.

57. Armand Mauss, *The Angel and the Beehive: The Mormon Struggle with Assimilation* (Urbana: University of Illinois Press, 1994), 84–85.

58. Dallin H. Oaks, "Alternate Voices," 1 Apr. 1989, https://www.churchof jesuschrist.org/study/general-conference/1989/04/alternate-voices?lang=eng, accessed 10 Feb. 2020.

Chapter 4. Reconciliation and Atonement

1. Eugene England, *Making Peace: Personal Essays (Salt Lake City: Signature Books, 1995)*, 87.

2. Eugene England, "Mormons and Watergate," *Dialogue: A Journal of Mormon Thought* 9.2 (Summer 1974): 65.

3. Reinhold Niebuhr, *The Children of Light and the Children of Darkness* (New York: Scribner, 1960), 84.

4. England, "Mormons and Watergate," 13–14.

5. Niebuhr, *The Children of Light and the Children of Darkness*, 129.

6. Ibid., 130.

7. Ibid.

8. England compares, with embarrassing hyperbole, the antipolygamy actions of the U.S. government to the Jim Crow laws and the internment of Japanese Americans during World War II.

9. Eugene England, "On Saving the Constitution: Why Some Utah Mormons Should Become Democrats," *Sunstone* 12:3 (May 1988): 23.

10. Eugene England, "The Weeping God of Mormonism," Dialogue: A Journal of Mormon Thought 35.1 (Spring 2002): 78.

11. Perhaps the most astute, and certainly the most amusing documentation of these cultural divisions was a column by Robert Kirby, published in *Sunstone* and later in the *Salt Lake Tribune*. Kirby divided Mormons into five types—1) "Conservative Mormons" ("the plump, short-haired Republican types with flowered dresses, suits, and bad breath that fill chapels each Sunday"); 2) "Orthodox Mormons" ("big on gospel trappings: temple tie-tacks, missionary name tags, and vinyl, American Tourister–size scripture covers. They adorn their homes with portraits of obscure general authorities and tole-painted crafts made in Relief Society"); 3) "Liberal Mormons" ("Regardless of temporal politics, L.M.s are considered liberal by virtue of their 'odd' or non-conformist notions about Mormonism . . . do not believe that every word that falls from the lips of a general authority represents the actual, personal opinion of Jesus Christ, . . . tend to worship most diligently at the altar of their own opinion. Unofficial Church policy and general membership consensus is that they are all going to hell"); 4) "Genuine Mormons" ("Genuine Mormons are practically invisible because of their low-key approach to the gospel. That and because they are rarely found at home, almost always being off helping others through some trial or other . . . operate out of love instead of guilt"); and 5) "Nazi Mormons" ("prone to long-winded and weepy testimony meeting claims about things that cannot be proven either in the world of science, logic, or even the scriptures, . . . not only believe everything a general authority utters, they will frequently take these counsels and improve on them. For example, if no single dating until the age of sixteen is good, no single dating until the draft age is even better"). Robert Kirby, "Five Kinds of Mormons," *Sunstone* 15.6 (Dec. 1991): 50–52.

12. William Whyte, *The Organization Man* (Philadelphia: University of Pennsylvania Press, 2002), 45–46.

13. Paul Tillich, *The Courage to Be*, 3rd ed. (New Haven: Yale University Press, 2014), 82.

14. Eugene England, "Obedience, Integrity, and the Paradox of Selfhood," *Dialogues with Myself* (Midvale, UT: Signature Books, 1984). Emphasis in original.

15. Unfortunately, it is always men—the usage here is deliberate.

16. England, *Dialogues with Myself*, 28.

17. Quoted in ibid., 29–31.

18. Some church authorities had taught, and many members believed, that people who were born Black were being punished for not having been valiant in defending God's ways in conflicts that occurred in a premortal existence.

19. England, *Dialogues with Myself*, 31.

20. England, "The Mormon Cross," *Dialogue: A Journal of Mormon Thought* 8.1 (Spring 1973): 82.

21. England, *Dialogues with Myself*, 35 (quoting Michael Novak, "The Family Out of Favor," *Harper's Magazine*, April 1976, 42).

22. Ibid.

23. Ibid., 104–5.

24. England, "'No Cause, No Cause,'" 37.

25. England, *Dialogues with Myself*, 72.

26. Ibid., 86.

27. Ibid. Emphasis in original. This, incidentally, is the point about which Neal Maxwell said that he was "not entirely persuaded," when England sent him the essay. See p. .

28. Articles of Faith: 2. (The Articles of Faith, now canonized as part of the Pearl of Great Price, were originally included in a letter written by Joseph Smith in 1842 to a newspaper editor named John Wentworth, requesting a brief outline of the history and beliefs of the Latter-day Saints.)

29. England, *Dialogues with Myself*, 80. N.B.: The Mormon scriptures England cites as warrant here portray *Eve, rather than Adam,* as the courageous seeker of wisdom: "And when the woman saw that the tree was good for food, and that it became pleasant to the eyes, and a tree to be desired to make her wise, she took of the fruit thereof, and did eat, and also gave unto her husband with her, and he did eat." Adam acknowledges her agency; when questioned by God, he replies: "The woman thou gavest me, and commandest that she should remain with me, she gave me of the fruit of the tree and I did eat." Moses 4:12, 18.

30. England, *Dialogues with Myself*, 87.

31. Eugene England, "Easter Weekend," *Dialogue: A Journal of Mormon Thought* 21.1 (Spring 1988): 22.

32. Stephen E. Robinson, "Believing Christ," https://www.churchofjesuschrist.org/study/ensign/1992/04/believing-christ?lang=eng, accessed 2 Jan. 2020.

33. Kent E. Robson, "Omnipotence, Omnipresence, and Omniscience in Mormon Theology," in *Line Upon Line: Essays on Mormon Doctrine*, ed. Gary Bergera (Salt Lake City: Signature Books, 1989), 71.

34. O. Kendall White, *Mormon Neo-Orthodoxy: A Crisis Theology* (Salt Lake City: Signature Books, 1987), 90.

35. J. Reuben Clark, *The Charted Course of the Church in Education* (Salt Lake City: Church of Jesus Christ of the Latter-day Saints, 2004), 10.

36. Douglas J. Davies, *The Mormon Culture of Salvation* (London: Routledge, 2000), 71.

37. Eugene England, "The Weeping God of Mormonism," *Dialogue: A Journal of Mormon Thought* 35.1 (Spring 2002): 75.

38. Ibid., 64.

39. Ibid., 65–66. Emphasis in original.

40. Ibid., 78.

41. Ibid., 79.

42. Fiona and Terryl Givens, *The God Who Weeps* (Salt Lake City: Ensign Peak, 2012), Kindle edition, location 343–58 (chap. 1)

43. England, "The Weeping God of Mormonism," 75.

44. Terry L. Givens, *Wrestling the Angel: The Foundations of Mormon Thought* (New York: Oxford University Press, 2014), 101.

Bibliographic Essay

1. Eugene England, "The Achievement of Lowell Bennion," *Sunstone* 12.4 (Jul. 1988): 24.

2. Eugene England, "Knowledge without Zeal," a statement on honors education at BYU given to the Humanities College faculty, 7 Dec. 1978, 6, eugeneengland.org/wp-content/uploads/sbi/articles/1978_sc_op_004.pdf.

3. Eugene England, "The Academic Study of Religion: Prospects and Perils," Aug. 2000. Audio available at https://sunstonemagazine.com/the-academic-study-of-religion-prospects-and-perils/. Cited in Charlotte Hansen Terry, "Eugene England's Calculated Risk," *Sunstone* 161 (Dec. 2010): 38–42.

4. Suzanne Lundquist, "Learning How to Learn," interview with Charlotte England, http://www.eugeneengland.org/eugene-england/remembering-gene-project/st-olaf-college-to-early-byu-career/learning-how-to-learn.

5. Eugene England, *Dialogues with Myself* (Midvale, UT: Signature Books, 1984), 183–84.

6. Margaret Young, " Hearing Gene's Voice," *Irreantum* 3.3 (Autumn 2001): 50.

7. All cited in Eugene England, "Mormon Literature: Progress and Prospects," *Irreantum* 3.3 (Autumn 2001): 68–69.

8. Ibid., 71.

9. Ibid., 89.

10. Ibid.

11. Eugene England, "Danger on the Right! Danger on the Left!: The Ethics of Recent Mormon Fiction," *Dialogue: A Journal of Mormon Thought* 32.3 (Fall 1999): 19.

12. Ibid., 28–29.

13. Eugene England, *Making Peace: Personal Essays* (Salt Lake City: Signature Books, 1995), 173.

14. Bruce R. McConkie, "All Are Alike unto God," address was given at the CES Religious Educators Symposium, 18 Apr. 1978, https://speeches.byu.edu/talks/bruce-r-mcconkie/alike-unto-god/, accessed 30 Jan. 2020.

15. Eugene England, "Becoming a World Religion: Blacks, the Poor—All of Us," *Sunstone* 21.2 (June/Jul. 1998): 49–60.

16. Richard Cracroft, Review of *Harvest: Contemporary Mormon Poems,* edited by Eugene England and Dennis Clark, *BYU Studies Quarterly* 30.2, article 15, https://scholarsarchive.byu.edu/byusq/vol30/iss2/15.

17. Richard Cracroft, "Eugene England and the Progress of Mormon Letters," *Sunstone* 121 (Jan. 2002): 44.

Index

134

KRISTINE L. HAGLUND is a writer, editor, and
independent scholar, and the former editor of
Dialogue: A Journal of Mormon Thought.

The University of Illinois Press
is a founding member of the
Association of University Presses.

University of Illinois Press
1325 South Oak Street
Champaign, IL 61820-6903
www.press.uillinois.edu